ENVIRONMENTAL PROBLEMS
GRASSROOTS SOLUTIONS

The Politics of Grassroots Environmental Conflict

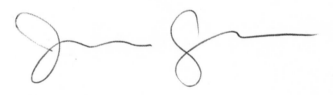

ENVIRONMENTAL PROBLEMS GRASSROOTS SOLUTIONS

The Politics of Grassroots Environmental Conflict

Sherry Cable

University of Tennessee—Knoxville

Charles Cable

St. Martin's Press

NEW YORK

Managing editor: Patricia Mansfield-Phelan
Project editor: Alda D. Trabucchi
Production supervisor: Joe Ford
Art director: Sheree Goodman
Cover design: Rod Hernandez

Library of Congress Catalog Card Number: 92-63065
Manufactured in the United States of America.
9 8 7 6 5
f e d c b a

For information, write:
St. Martin's Press, Inc.
175 Fifth Avenue
New York, NY 10010

ISBN: 0-312-08142-1

To Katy Cable,
of course,
and in memory of Rini.

Preface

Environmental Problems / Grassroots Solutions is a response to the lack of an adequate text on the sociological aspects of environmental problems. After several years of using an anthology of readings for a sociology course on environmental issues, we wanted to develop a textbook that would bring our perspective to the classroom. We wanted to demonstrate that beyond the technical issues, environmental problems are social; specifically, they are the products of human decisions and the resolutions of human conflicts.

To date, no single, overarching perspective unifies the field of environmental sociology to the degree found, for example, in criminology or demography. Indeed, nearly as many approaches exist as do people claiming to be environmental sociologists. Whereas some analysts focus on the creation and enforcement of environmental policies and some on the energy crunch, others examine the degree of environmental concern among the public. The topics that a conscientious teacher of environmental sociology may cover encompass a tremendous range, including the consequences of population growth for the environment; technological development; the role of religion in shaping environmental attitudes; the nuclear industry; social impact assessment; risk assessment; urban society; human ecology; and the effects of modern industrialization on the environment. Consequently, a variety of valid approaches might be taken in the sociological study of environmental issues. No solid consensus on a theoretical base for environmental sociology currently exists, and the ambiguity resulting from this theoretical vacuum has persistently undermined the legitimacy of the study area.

At this point in the development of the field, the most reasonable strategy is to develop theories and orientations within specific subareas, in the hope of eventually attaining some coherence. Since our greatest interest and knowledge lie in grassroots environmental conflict, we focus on that subarea. We certainly make no attempt to provide the generic and atheoretical cataloging of environmental problems, which is best left to comprehensive publications such as World Watch Institute's *State of the World* series, the *Global Ecology Handbook,* and similar efforts.

We begin *Environmental Problems / Grassroots Solutions* with a discussion of the need for sociologists to be involved in identifying and solving environmental problems; then Chapter 2 provides a detailed account of the political economy view of environmental issues. Through this analysis we provide an explanation of grassroots environmental conflict. In Chapter 3, we ground the political economy perspective of environmental conflict by discussing the specific links between the expansion of industrial production and some principles of ecosystem function. In deference to the social science students who typically lack a strong physical science background, our discussion includes an environmental science primer that has been class-tested.

Next, in Chapter 4, we analyze how the corporate state structure acts to expand industrial production, with the frequent result of contaminated communities. After providing a history of the relationship between economic growth and environmental exploitation in the United States (Chapter 5), we document (Chapter 6) the beginning of citizens' questioning of the costs and benefits of economic growth—the Love Canal and Three Mile Island disasters that led to environmental grassroots conflict. Finally, we examine the environmental injustices that generate grassroots environmental organizations (Chapter 8) and the organizations' subsequent quests for broader environmental justice (Chapter 9).

This text specifically targets undergraduate students in environmental sociology courses. In addition, it may be used as a supplemental text in social problems for instructors who prefer an in-depth approach focusing on several social problems rather than a kaleidoscope of social ills. The text may also serve as a supplement for graduate-level courses in environmental sociology in which grassroots environmental conflict is included among other related topics such as environmental regulation, the environmental movement, and environmental attitudes.

Instructors may use the text for selected advanced undergraduate courses in sociology. For example, they might emphasize the unequal distribution of environmental problems in a social stratification course or the role of the state in setting and enforcing environmental policies in courses in conflict resolution or environmental policy. A course in technology and society might employ the book as context for the discussion of the relationship between decisions on technological innovations and the fragility of democratic processes.

Instructors of courses in other social sciences might also find the book useful. An emphasis on the social forces that shape environmental decisions and environmental use might be welcome in courses in social ecology, cultural anthropology, psychology, and economics.

We even entertain the hope that the text will be used to supplement courses in environmental science, geology, biology, geography, agriculture, forestry, and other areas. Environmental issues are inherently multidisciplinary. If people are eventually to understand and resolve the world's environmental problems—*our* environmental problems—we must work together and share our knowledge rather than indulge in petty jurisdictional disputes over knowledge domains.

Instructors may wish to supplement their courses by having students work with EcoNet. EcoNet is a computer bulletin-board system, the "environmental network," founded in 1987 to facilitate communication among environmentalists in over seventy countries. It is an environmental news source and a worldwide environmental conference center. News contributors include the Sierra Club, Friends of the Earth, and Greenpeace. For more information, see Don Rittner's *EcoLinking: Everyone's Guide to Online Environmental Information* (Peachpit Press, 1992), or contact the Institute for Global Communications (415/442-0220) at 18 de Boom, San Francisco, California 94107.

Acknowledgments

We are grateful to a number of people for their various types of assistance in this project. Professor Chip Hastings, Sherry's friend and colleague at the University of Tennessee–Knoxville, provided encouragement, consultation, and his considerable editing talents in shaping earlier drafts of this manuscript. We acknowledge the important contributions of students in Sherry's undergraduate and graduate environmental sociology classes over the last seven years whose responses (positive and negative) had a great influence on the structure and theoretical foundation of this book. No one gets very far in writing a textbook without significant assistance by clerical staff, and we extend a special thanks to the office staff in the Department of Sociology: Karen Jones, Linda Robinson, and Virginia Carey. Although the thoughts and ideas in this book are not meant to represent anyone but us, we express deep gratitude to and respect for grassroots environmental activists everywhere, but particularly to those in the Yellow Creek Valley of southeastern Kentucky who taught us that environmental issues are fundamentally social class issues: thank you Larry and Shelia Wilson, Hotense Quillen, and Gene and Viola Hurst. May your grandchildren—and all our grandchildren—fish in clear streams.

Sherry Cable
Charles Cable

Contents

Chronology of Important Environmental Events

1681	William Penn issues ordinance that for every 5 acres of land cleared 1 acre must be left forested.
1710	The Massachusetts Colony enacts laws to protect waterfowl in the coastal areas.
1832	U.S. cholera epidemic kills hundreds.
1849	The U.S. Department of the Interior is established.
1850	U.S. cholera epidemic kills hundreds.
1859	Charles Darwin's *The Origin of Species* is published.
1864	The Yosemite Valley is reserved as a state park.
1866	U.S. cholera epidemic kills hundreds.
1871	The U.S. Fish Commission is established.
	Massive fire in Wisconsin is caused by exploitative logging practices.
1872	Yellowstone National Park is established.
1873	U.S. cholera epidemic kills hundreds.
1875	American Forestry Association is organized.
1876	Appalachian Mountain Club is formed.
1879	The U.S. Geological Survey is established.
1881	The Division of Forestry is created.
1885	Niagara Falls is protected by law.
	The Boone and Crockett Club is formed.
1886	The New York Audubon Society is organized.

Source: This environmental chronology has been compiled from several sources, most significantly Roderick Frazier Nash, *American Environmentalism: Readings in Conservation History,* 3rd ed. (New York: McGraw-Hill, 1990); and G. Tyler Miller, Jr., *Environmental Science: An Introduction,* second edition (Belmont, Calif.: Wadsworth, 1988).

1889   Devastating flood in Johnstown, Pennsylvania, caused by exploitative logging practices.

1890   The U.S. Census Bureau announces the closing of the American frontier.

1891   The Forest Reserve Act is passed, which allows the president to establish national forests on public domains.

Yosemite National Park is established.

1892   The Sierra Club is organized.

1894   Devastating fire in Minnesota is caused by exploitative logging practices.

1897   The Forest Management Act is passed.

1899   The River and Harbor Act is passed, which is the first law to ban the pollution of navigable waters.

1902   The Bureau of Reclamation is created.

1905   The National Audubon Society is organized.

1906   The Antiquities Act is passed.

1908   The Grand Canyon is made a national monument.

1913   After battles with conservationists, part of Yosemite National Park is granted to the city of San Francisco for a reservoir.

1916   The National Park Service Act is passed.

1920   The Mineral Leasing Act is passed, which regulates mining on federal lands.

The Federal Water Power Act is passed, which allows the government to issue licenses for the development of hydropower.

1922   The Izaak Walton League is formed.

1924   The Oil Pollution Control Act is passed.

The government declares a wilderness area in the Gila National Forest in New Mexico.

1928   The government authorizes the Hoover Dam project.

1933   The Civilian Conservation Corps is created.

The Tennessee Valley Authority is established.

1935   The Wilderness Society is organized.

1936   The National Wildlife Federation is established.

1940   The U.S. Fish and Wildlife Service is established.

1942   The federal government's Manhattan Project begins planning and construction of plants for developing the world's first atomic bomb. Major plants are located at Oak Ridge, Tennessee; Hanford, Washington; and Los Alamos, New Mexico.

1945   The United States drops "Little Boy," the world's first atomic bomb, on Hiroshima, Japan.

1946   The U.S. Bureau of Land Management is formed to administer the public domain.

The Atomic Energy Act is passed, which limits private ownership of fissionable materials and provides for civilian rather than military control over the development of nuclear warheads and naval reactors.

1948   The Federal Water Pollution Control Law is passed to regulate waste disposal.

Air pollution kills 20 people in Donora, Pennsylvania.

1952   Air pollution kills 4000 in London.

The federal government founds the Lawrence Livermore National Laboratory in Livermore, California, to develop and test hydrogen bombs.

1956   The Water Pollution Control Act is passed to provide federal grants to cities for water treatment plants.

1960   The Multiple Use-Sustained Yield Act is passed.

Dwight D. Eisenhower warns nation against the military-industrial complex.

1962   Rachel Carson's *Silent Spring* is published.

1963   The Clean Air Act is passed.

1964   The Wilderness Act is passed which establishes the National Wilderness Preservation System.

1966   The Endangered Species Act is passed.

Eighty people die in New York City from pollution-related causes during a four-day inversion.

1967   The Environmental Defense Fund is formed.

1968   Paul Ehrlich's *The Population Bomb* is published.

The National Wild and Scenic Rivers Act and the National Trails System Act are passed.

The astronauts photograph "Spaceship Earth."

1969   The Santa Barbara oil spill occurs.

The Cuyahoga River catches fire in Cleveland, Ohio.

Friends of Earth is organized.

Greenpeace is founded.

1970   The National Environmental Policy Act is passed.

The Natural Resources Defense Council is established.

Zero Population Growth is organized.

The Clean Air Act is passed, which is more stringent than the 1963 law.

The first Earth Day is celebrated.

The Environmental Protection Agency is established.

1971   Barry Commoner's *The Closing Circle* is published.

The Alaska Native Claims Settlement Act is passed, which permits government to protect "national interest lands."

1972   The League of Conservation Voters is created.

The Clean Water Act is passed.

The EPA develops a permit system for toxic chemicals; citizens receive the right to sue corporate violators.

The Federal Environmental Pesticide Control Act is passed.

The Ocean Dumping Act is passed.

The Coastal Zone Management Act is passed.

The United Nations Conference on the Human Environment is held in Sweden.

The Limits of Growth is published.

1973   E. F. Schumacher's *Small Is Beautiful* is published.

The OPEC oil embargo is announced.

The Endangered Species Act is passed.

Congressional approval is obtained to build an 800-mile oil pipeline across Alaska.

1974   The Safe Drinking Water Act is passed.

Congress splits the Atomic Energy Commission into the Nuclear Regulatory Commission and the Energy Research and Development Administration.

1976 The Federal Land Policy and Management Act is passed which governs the multiple use of public lands.

The Resource Conservation and Recovery Act is passed.

The Toxic Substances Control Act is passed.

1977 Amendments are added to the Clean Air Act.

The Energy Research and Development Administration lasts only three years; President Jimmy Carter replaces it with the Department of Energy.

Amendments are added to the Clean Water Act.

The Surface Mining Control and Reclamation Act is passed.

1978 The National Energy Act is passed.

President Jimmy Carter issues an executive order instructing the military to comply with environmental legislation. The order was not enforced.

The Love Canal landfill is deemed "a grave and imminent peril" to residents.

1979 A partial meltdown occurs in a nuclear reactor at the Three Mile Island nuclear generating plant.

Midland, Michigan, residents trace illnesses to dioxin-contaminated air produced at the Dow Chemical factory.

1980 The Comprehensive Environmental Response, Compensation and Liability Act (CERCLA) is passed, creating the Superfund program for five years.

Another National Energy Act is passed.

1981 Ronald Reagan takes office as president and begins policies of environmental deregulation.

Lois Gibbs founds the Citizen's Clearinghouse for Hazardous Wastes.

Earth First! is established.

1983 Times Beach, Missouri, is abandoned because of dioxin contamination.

1984   An industrial accident at the Union Carbide chemical plant in Bhopal, India, kills more than 2000 people.

The Cerrell Report is released, an industry study identifying the demographic characteristics of the neighborhoods most and least resistant to hazardous waste facilities in their communities.

The Safe Drinking Water Act is passed.

1985   A major leak of toxic chemicals occurs at the Union Carbide plant in Institute, West Virginia.

CERCLA expires, ending the Superfund program.

1986   The explosion and fire occurs at the Chernobyl nuclear plant in the Ukraine.

The Superfund program is reauthorized through the Superfund Amendments and Reauthorization Act (SARA).

1987   The Clean Water Act is passed.

The Commission for Racial Justice, appointed by the United Church of Christ, releases its report, "Toxic Wastes and Race: A National Report on the Racial and Socioeconomic Characteristics of Communities with Hazardous Wastes," documenting environmental racism.

1988   Michael Dukakis and George Bush vie for the title of "Most Serious Environmentalist"; Bush wins.

The Department of Energy releases its plan for rebuilding and cleaning up the military's weapons complex.

1989   A huge oil spill occurs in Prince William Sound, Alaska.

1990   The second Earth Day is celebrated around the globe.

1992   The United Nations sponsors the Earth Summit in Rio de Janeiro, the first world conference on environmental problems.

Environmentalist and U.S. Senator Albert Gore elected as vice president.

Congress passes the Federal Facilities Act that puts federal facilities, including the military, under the same environmental enforcement regimen as the civilian sector.

1993   The EPA has identified more than 2000 toxic waste storage sites that must be cleaned up to protect residents.

ENVIRONMENTAL PROBLEMS
GRASSROOTS SOLUTIONS

The Politics of Grassroots Environmental Conflict

1. Of Environmental Sociology and the Butterfly Effect

Signs of environmental stress abound. Nonproductive farmlands, eroded hillsides, overgrazed grasslands, and denuded mountain ranges are in evidence worldwide. Each year approximately 17 million hectares of tropical forest—an area the size of Oklahoma—vanish. Water and air quality is deteriorating, becoming life-threatening instead of life-sustaining. Fish catches are diminishing. Nearly half of all African nations face catastrophic food shortages. By the year 2000, the average rate of species extinction is expected to be 20,000 species a year, or one species every thirty minutes. Cities worldwide are drowning in their own garbage and shrouded in photochemical smog. According to estimates by the U.S. Department of Energy, 80 percent of the world's known reserves of crude oil will be depleted by the year 2013. The U.S. Environmental Protection Agency estimates that only about 10 percent of the hazardous wastes produced in the United States are disposed of properly. The agency has identified more than 2000 toxic waste storage sites that must be cleaned up to protect residents from illness or death.

Fortunately, signs of greater environmental awareness are also becoming apparent. In the United States, newspapers, periodicals, and television are covering environmental issues with greater frequency, alerting people to the potential dangers of global warming, acid rain, deforestation, chemical waste dumps, and the municipal garbage crisis. Network newscasts often feature week-long series on environmental issues. Analyses of opinion polls show that public concern with environmental quality increased significantly and steadily in the 1980s, both in terms of awareness of the "seriousness" of environmental problems and support for environmental protection. The environment was a key issue, at least in rhetoric, during the 1988 U.S. presidential campaign, as candidates George Bush and Michael Dukakis vied for the title of "Most Serious Environmentalist." Public concern about the environment reached the highest levels ever by the time of Earth Day in 1990. This celebration of the planet was marked by some 100 million participants in over 100 countries. In November 1992

1

Americans elected the Democratic ticket of Bill Clinton and recognized environmentalist Albert Gore to lead the country. A twenty-two-nation Gallup poll found that a majority of people in sixteen nations, including some of the world's poorest, claimed they would willingly pay higher prices so that industry could better protect the environment.

Perhaps the most significant environmental event in recent years was the Earth Summit in 1992. In June of that year, the United Nations sponsored the first world conference on environmental problems in Rio de Janeiro. It was the largest assembly of heads of state meeting about the environment in history, drawing 118 heads of state, more than 9000 news reporters, and some 15,000 participants representing nongovernmental organizations from 165 nations.

With such attention directed to environmental issues, it is tempting to think that solutions for our environmental problems are just around the next corner. However, such resolution requires much more than awareness, much more than the sincere wish to be free of environmental problems. Before we can devise solutions for our environmental problems, we must first understand them and examine their root causes. What does such an understanding require?

Many people view environmental problems in purely technical terms, as problems that require only the expertise of physical scientists. After all, environmental problems are clearly physical problems that occur in physical systems. Biologists, chemists, geologists, and engineers are ingenious enough to effect change after change in the physical system. So, many people reason, if we change the environment in a way that hurts us, we will recognize our error, develop new technological marvels, and change the environment back to what it was. For several reasons, it will not be that simple.

The physical problems themselves resist easy solutions. The environment is not a passive object that we can shape at will. The environment is alive, it operates on its own terms, and it is incomprehensibly complex. We can neither identify nor estimate the probabilities of the almost infinite possible ramifications of our making one deliberate change in the environment. For example, we think we can add a chemical to surface water and call it safe for drinking. In truth, however, the effects of the chemical depend in complicated ways on factors including water temperature, water current, rainfall, the presence of other chemicals in the water, and a host of other influences that cannot be measured or are as yet unrecognized.

This complexity is suggested by the concept called the Butterfly Effect. The *Butterfly Effect* refers to a belief, half-jokingly held among weather forecasters, that a butterfly taking off today in Beijing can affect next month's weather in New York. This concept, more accurately referred to as "sensitive dependence on initial conditions," is described by James Gleick in his popular book, *Chaos: Making a New Science* (1987): "For small pieces of weather—and to a global forecaster, small can mean thunderstorms and blizzards—any prediction deteriorates rapidly. Errors and uncertainties multiply, cascading upward through a chain of turbulent features, from dust devils and squalls to continent-size eddies that only satellites can see" (1987:20).

The Butterfly Effect is offered as an explanation for the inaccuracy of weather forecasts as they are projected further into the future. Forecasts for two to three days in advance tend to be fairly accurate; they then deteriorate to educated speculations. Even using the most powerful and sophisticated computers, weather forecasts are virtually worthless beyond six or seven days (and not necessarily because of butterflies taking wing in Beijing). In fact, computational power is irrelevant, since no method of data collection could ever be as sensitive as the system itself.

The idea of sensitive dependence on initial conditions is widely applicable to many physical systems and can be stated in this way: Tiny differences in input can quickly become overwhelming differences in output. In a system as vast as the support of life on earth, the tiny differences in initial conditions are nearly infinite, far too vast even to be known, let alone controlled. We can, therefore, never hope to predict accurately the ultimate effects of even small acts of human intervention.

Many natural systems now seem to fit the general chaos model, including weather, air and water currents, the rise and fall of animal populations, and measles epidemics. If it proves to be a useful model of the environment and its response to pollution, then other aspects of chaos may be relevant, such as the phenomenon called turbulence. The behavior of fluids is predictable as long as flow remains smooth and orderly. If stress to the system is increased, however, a point is reached when the orderly flow breaks up into unstable disorder. The transition point cannot be accurately predicted, even in a system as simple as smoke rising from a cigarette. And once the transition point has been passed, the system behaves quite differently and unpredictably.

The implications for major environmental systems are ominous. We intuitively expect the response of the system to change in steady proportion to the stress applied to it. But the system may reach a point at which the change in response is sudden and discontinuous, resulting in conditions that are calamitous, unpredictable, and much more difficult to control. Chaos, complexity, and the inclusion of smaller-scale irreversibilities, from strip mining to species extinction, make large-scale reversibility impossible.

The physical unpredictability and irreversibility of the environment means that intervention by physical science cannot be regarded as a dependable safety net, cannot be counted on to save us. The technological marvels needed to accomplish such magic have not been and never will be devised, and we are confronted with an environment that our own manipulations have made hostile to us. While it is certainly true that environmental problems occur when ecological principles are violated and that dealing with such violations requires a knowledge of biology, geology, and the other physical sciences, the problem is not merely a technical problem, best left to the physical scientists.

Both initially and ultimately, environmental problems are social problems. Certainly, many physical solutions already known could be done immediately, but many people believe the cost outweighs the danger. The real hope of those who believe in Technology as Savior is that science will find a solution that is neither costly nor inconvenient. More than anything else, it is this restriction on physical science that makes environmental degradation a social problem.

Think about water and air pollution, about the disposal of toxic wastes. All living things are affected by these problems, but who is it who violates ecological principles and causes environmental problems? People. And who can do something about the problems? Only people. People can effect changes in the environment easily enough, but we cannot fully predict what they will be and we will not necessarily survive them. The question of human survival makes environmental problems *social* problems. Thus, environmental problems are social in nature by virtue of both their origins and their consequences.

WHY SOCIOLOGY?

In a 1991 hearing before the Committee on Environmental Research of the National Research Council, environmental sociologist William Freudenberg testified:

> While your committee faces a problem that in many ways is as complex as it is important, I intend to address the problem by making just a single point, and one that is deceptively simple. If you reflect for a moment about virtually all of the testimony you are receiving, not just from me, but also from other speakers, you will find that the problems tend to reflect the behaviors of a single species—*homo sapiens*. My central point is that . . . one of the most pressing needs for *environmental* research is in the need for better understanding of the *human and institutional* factors that tend to be the real, root causes of the problems (reprinted in *Environment, Technology, and Society*, Summer 1992:1).

Why sociology rather than another social science? All social sciences study human behavior. For any particular behavior, we could devise explanations that involve the individual's inherited traits, dispositional characteristics, personality quirks, family background, friendship networks, occupation, social class, and so on. All of these explanations are "true"; that is, they all contribute to an understanding of the individual's behavior. Over the years, however, so much knowledge about human behavior has accumulated that no one discipline can contain all of it. Consequently, a division of labor occurred, creating separate disciplines that focus on the same general phenomenon—human behavior—but that concentrate on particular types of explanations for it—for example, psychological and sociological. The particular types of explanations characterizing each discipline represent distinctly different analytical perspectives.

The perspectives are not mutually exclusive. Each is valid and can be used to address environmental issues. Sociology offers a unique perspective on these issues, however, one that people use far less in their everyday lives than a psychological perspective.

Sociology is the scientific study of society, particularly the study of individuals in groups and organizations. A sociological view of environmental issues examines the societal sources of environmental problems—our expectations and values and the ways in which we organize things to meet those expectations. In other words, sociologists study the cultural and structural sources of environmental problems. From this perspective, environmental problems are not caused by evil persons, greedy business executives, or by any particular *type* of individual at all. Instead, dominant cultural beliefs and social institutions, the organizations in society that reflect and reinforce those beliefs, are responsible for environmental degradation, as well as the failure to address the problem. *Environmental sociology*, then, examines people's beliefs about the environment, their behavior toward it, and the ways in which the structure of society influences them and contributes to the persistent abuse of the environment.

Abuse of the environment does not just happen. People decide how to use the environment, but they do not decide simply on some objective basis of right and wrong, safe and unsafe. Instead, decisions on environmental use are reached in a social context: they are influenced by such factors as cultural values and attitudes toward the environment, social class, and our relationships to others. Disagreement among social groups over environmental use and what constitutes "right" and "safe" sometimes erupts into social conflict. Thus, environmental issues frequently become arenas of conflict in which social groups with varying levels of power each vie for public acceptance of their particular interpretation of the situation consonant with their own interests.

In this book, we focus on those conflicts associated with definitions of environmental problems. In many ways, these grassroots environmental conflicts are similar to other kinds of social conflict among groups of differing power. So, environmental sociologists use environmental issues to demonstrate the social organization and resource distribution dynamics that routinely operate within society.

Grassroots environmental conflicts begin at the local, or grassroots, level. That is, ordinary, everyday people with relatively little political power become concerned about some environmental threat to their community. Let's take a quick look at this conflict by using a hypothetical example.

A CASE OF CONFLICT

A few residents of Smalltowne, USA, notice that the Lovely River running through town does not seem to be what it was. They begin to grumble about the way the water smells and looks. Several persistent souls track the source of the water pollution to the Smalltowne Paper Mill, whose waste products, they discover, are dumped directly into the Lovely River. Some of the angry residents then join together to form a citizens organization, Smalltowne Concerned Citizens. Smalltowne Concerned Citizens (SCC) is a grassroots organization because it is initiated by people from the lower, rather than the higher, rungs of the social ladder. SCC members spread word of the source of the water pollution among other community residents. They write to their congressional representatives and petition the Smalltowne mayor and city council to stop the paper mill's dumping of waste products into the Lovely River. At this point, SCC members believe that simply making officials aware that a water problem exists will resolve the threat.

Instead, SCC members find that the mayor and city council minimize the seriousness of the water pollution. Conflict erupts between the local political authorities and the grassroots activists over whose definitions of "environmental harm" will determine policies. SCC members are shocked to discover that the very officials they elected to represent their interests and preserve the public welfare do not, in fact, represent them. The experience is a politicizing—even radicalizing—one for these patriotic citizens with strong beliefs in democracy.

The Smalltowne activists try to build a consensus within city government on their definition of environmental harm by seeking experts to testify on the likely negative health effects of the polluted Lovely River. But they discover that the Smalltowne Paper Mill is important to the mayor and the city council. Strict adherence to environmental laws would be expensive for the paper mill, whose executives predict they would be forced to lay off workers which, in turn, could send Smalltowne's economy into a slide that would push the mayor and city council members right out of office in the next election. Backed by the local authorities, the owners of the paper mill have much more political power than does the SCC and consequently a greater likelihood of maintaining their own definition of environmental harm.

Therefore, what the SCC lacks in economic power, it must compensate for with increased political power—in a word: votes. The group's efforts turn from persuading authorities to recruiting additional group members. SCC membership grows by word of mouth as members convince relatives, friends, neighbors, and co-workers to join their cause. With a larger mass base, activists organize protest demonstrations and sit-ins. State officials intervene and hold public hearings in Smalltowne on the water pollution issue. The hearings generate publicity in the media, and SCC gains more sympathizers. In a nonbinding referendum vote, Smalltowne residents vote overwhelmingly to force the owners of the paper mill to comply with existing environmental regulations.

The SCC is not without its critics, however. Workers at the paper mill criticize the SCC for being "radical" from fear that the mill will make good its latest threat to close down and move the entire operation to "a community that will appreciate the prosperity we bring," leaving them unemployed. Environmentalists, Inc., a national environmental lobbying organization, offers to help the SCC—but only if members defer to them about strategies and organizational structure. Also opposed to the SCC's cause are several businesses whose revenues depend directly on the paper mill—a supplier of safety apparel worn by the workers, a trucking firm that transports lumber to the paper mill, and a tavern located just across the street from the paper mill.

When state-ordered public hearings on the pollution of the Lovely River bring no resolution to the environmental conflict, SCC turns next to the courts. Members hire lawyers and other experts in fields such as biology, chemistry, geology, and engineering, and they raise funds for their efforts by sponsoring raffles, bake sales, and barbecues. As litigation becomes their dominant strategy, some group members drop out because their participation is now limited to interpreting lawyers' arguments. Responsibility for the cause falls on the shoulders of a small cadre of activists who are willing and able to pursue litigation for several years.

In the end, the Lovely River is significantly cleaner but not really clean. The Smalltowne Paper Mill has been forced to expend some profits on compliance with environmental regulations but not so much that many jobs are lost. Visible change has occurred in the community, but perhaps the most important change is not as immediately apparent as is the relatively cleaner water of the Lovely River.

The most significant change in the community is more social than physical. Regardless of their levels of satisfaction with the resolution of the environmental problem, SCC members will never be the same. They are disillusioned with the political system. What happened to the will of the majority? They vow never again to allow the will of the people to be subjugated to economic interests. Several of them run for city council and win on a platform encouraging greater political participation. Therefore, SCC members' efforts to correct a local water quality problem led them to a quest for environmental justice and a political consciousness that challenges cherished cultural ideals.

THE TRUTH HURTS

Unfortunately, this same drama can be played out in thousands of communities across the United States. Here are but a few examples.

- For over a decade, a 2400-acre site in Alabama run by the world's largest waste disposal company has taken in 500,000 tons of hazardous wastes per year while leaking pesticides and volatile solvents into nearby communities. Traces of the chemicals have appeared in local wells and allegedly contributed to serious health problems.

- For fifteen years a uranium conversion facility in Oklahoma allowed uranium dust to drift into the surrounding neighborhoods and dumped liquid wastes directly into the nearby rivers, contaminating fish, wildlife, and vegetation.

- In the early 1970s, residents of a small Michigan town noted an increasing incidence of birth defects that ranged from cleft palates to heart malformations. By the late 1970s, some farm families reported strange deformities afflicting animals, including cows and horses losing their hair in clumps and rabbits growing huge tumors. Residents reported skin rashes, nosebleeds, headaches, immunological diseases, miscarriages, brain tumors, respiratory illnesses, and uterine cancer. The problems were eventually traced to dioxin-contaminated air, produced at the Dow Chemical factory along with Agent Orange, the defoliant used in the Vietnam War.

In each case, political authorities and corporate executives were reluctant to take citizens' complaints seriously enough to thoroughly investigate their claims. In each case, the poisoning of the environment—and people—continued. And in each case, grassroots environmental movements arose and conflict erupted over the definition of environmental harm.

In the last ten years, grassroots environmental conflicts have captured the imagination of sociological researchers. Much of the work the researchers have thus far produced is descriptive without a consistent theoretical base. Yet, an examination of conflict is central in sociological theories about many social phenomena: political processes, international relations, small group behavior, racism, stratification, socialization, and many other phenomena. We can gain some understanding of grassroots environmental conflicts by using theories from this extensive sociological tradition.

A focus on conflict draws attention to inequalities in society. Social classes are an important set of categories in sociological studies, representing inequalities in the way power, privilege, and prestige are distributed in society. Different social classes are likely to hold different values and beliefs about what is fair in the distribution of benefits and who should have access to the better things in life. Conflicts between individuals in different classes often result over such values and beliefs.

Environmental problems may be seen in much the same way, for they, too, are unevenly distributed in society. All human activities take place in a spatial area, and the use of space is socially determined. Those who have greater power, privilege, and prestige are more influential in the political arena where decisions are made. They assign favorable environmental conditions to themselves and unfavorable conditions to people with less power, privilege, and prestige. Translation: The lower the social class of an individual, the more likely the individual is to live and work in an area with environmental problems. Thus, environmental problems are similar to other kinds of inequalities and have the potential to generate conflicts between social groups. The inherently political processes shaping environmental policies and decision-making processes make the focus on environmental conflicts a logical place to begin work on a comprehensive theoretical foundation for the field of environmental sociology.

Through its focus on conflict and the sociological tools of the trade, this book raises questions about a fundamental value in society: the belief in democratic processes. How do grassroots environmental conflicts relate to democracy and to social change? Such conflicts pit a small, powerful social group against a larger, less powerful, social group, and the resulting interaction between power and numbers raises fundamental issues about the workings of a democratic nation. In the United States, the belief in democratic processes permeates the culture. The "rule of the majority" is a basic value. Does this value disappear at the community level? Do we suspend democratic procedures where economic interests are at stake? How do our social institutions produce environmental problems and block efforts to ameliorate them? This book will address such issues, not by analyzing the individuals who make the decisions affecting the environment but, rather, by examining the social and political contexts in which these decisions are made.

2. *The Environment According to Sociology*

Over 2000 years ago, Aristotle asserted that humans are by nature social animals. We are, first and foremost, social creatures who live our entire lives with others more or less like ourselves. We cannot be human alone; we influence and are influenced by others through interaction in group settings. Sociology examines these influences and social settings, as well as all the meanings, expectations, behaviors, and social arrangements that emerge from people interacting in society. Indeed, the focus of sociology is the human social experience. The sociological perspective increases our understanding of how social relationships in society are structured, how power is distributed, and how beliefs and social forces guide our behavior.

In this chapter, we establish the analytical framework we will use in the remainder of the book. We begin with a review of some basic sociology that is relevant to environmental issues; then, building on those fundamentals, we present our political economy perspective on grassroots environmental conflict.

A SOCIOLOGICAL VIEW OF ENVIRONMENTAL ISSUES

Social institutions are formalized systems of beliefs and behavior composed of interrelated cultural norms that provide established answers and standardized solutions for the basic social tasks necessary to sustain society. These essential tasks include the production and distribution of goods and services. Production is dependent on the physical environment: *everything* that is produced is derived from the physical environment, and *everything* that is discarded is returned to the environment in a different form.

The institution most directly connected to production processes is the economic institution. The institution in which the powerful exert their influence over the distribution of goods and services in society is the political institution. Most contemporary political and economic institutions—under both capitalism and socialism—are designed to depend critically on constantly increasing rates of economic growth to support increasing standards of living. *Economic growth* refers to increases in the capacity of the economy to provide goods and services for final use.

Culture consists of the shared ideas, values, and beliefs that together provide a kind of blueprint for appropriate behavior in the group. Cultural values both reflect and reinforce institutional structures. Thus, we have not only political and economic institutions that encourage ever-increasing economic growth, but also reinforcing cultural values and ideologies that permeate other social institutions. For example, schools propagate the value of Technology as Savior and the implicit assumption that the supply of resources is infinite, and some religions teach that the physical world was created expressly for exploitation by humans. These values contribute to the depletion of resources and the reliance on technology to resolve depletion problems.

Some individuals and social groups have disproportionate influence on the components of culture. Those who stand to gain the most through the existing social and cultural system also have the power to perpetuate that system through legislation, values, customs, and their greater access to decision-making processes. They have the power, then, to impose their definitions of "right" and "dangerous" on the rest of society. If they are disposed *not* to view a situation as an environmental problem, they have the ability to bring powerful social forces, including the government, to bear on their side. Thus, the powerful remain powerful.

Consequently, environmental problems derive from two sources: cultural and institutional. The cultural sources of environmental problems are the beliefs and ideologies that reinforce the social structure in a society, including

- *The belief that a free market system provides the greatest good for the greatest number of people.* This value leads us to place economic decision-making processes in private hands. Frequently, however, such private decisions have public consequences.

- *The belief that the natural world is inexhaustible.* This belief contributes to overconsumption and the waste of resources. Products are deliberately planned to become obsolete within a relatively short time so that consumers will buy new ones. Americans recycle very little and reuse even less. We continually reduce the diversity of plant and animal life, leading to problems such as species extinction, soil erosion, and flooding.

- *A faith in technology.* It is part of our cultural heritage to believe that technology can meet any challenge. People regard themselves as ingenious creatures who will be able to devise solutions for any problems. But technology itself, if not sufficiently controlled (and complete control is not humanly possible), can speed degradation of the earth's life support system.

- *The growth ethic.* This is the belief that growth equals progress, that bigger is always better. We believe that the more we produce and consume, the better off we are. Consequently, we deemphasize sustainable forms of economic growth.

- *Materialism.* Americans consistently measure success in terms of the consumption of material things. We believe that the most important nation is the one that can command and use the largest fraction of the world's resources.

- *The value of individualism.* American values emphasize individual rights and personal achievement. We place benefits to the self above benefits to the collective. As a consequence, we admire the person who makes a fortune by extracting raw resources and producing goods with economic efficiency, and we pay little attention to the social costs.

- *Our anthropocentric worldview.* We see the world as being centered around people, and we believe that people are superior to all other species. Standing *apart from* nature rather than recognizing that we are *a part of* nature, we attempt to conquer and subdue the environment.

Institutional sources of environmental problems are the patterned behaviors that contribute to environmental problems. They involve the structural arrangements in society that buttress the belief system and reinforce the abuse of the environment. Institutional sources of environmental problems include the economic and political institutions.

Economy refers to the production and distribution of goods and services in society. Decisions must be made concerning what to produce, in what quantities, by what method, and for whom. The economic institution affects resource use and environmental quality because producing anything requires resources and has some negative impact on the environment. In capitalist systems, decisions about economic matters are made in the private sphere because of values regarding ownership and private property. The decisions, then, reflect the interests of the decision makers themselves, the property owners. Property owners endeavor to maximize their private profits.

Consequently, economic decisions result in environmental problems and the *externalization of the environmental costs of production.* This means that the costs of production's negative impact on the environment (for example, the costs of cleaning polluted water to make it suitable for drinking) are not included in the price of the product. The company neither pays for the privilege of polluting the water nor cleans it; it saves the cost of proper waste disposal and makes environmentally conscious competition impossible. Not even the consumer of the product pays the environmental costs of production directly. Rather, the public at large essentially subsidizes the company, by either paying for the cleanup of the environment or enduring degraded environmental quality.

Political systems are social arrangements that define and defend the use and distribution of power within a society. *Power* refers to the ability of individuals and groups to realize their will in human affairs even if it encounters the resistance of others. The polity determines the use and distribution of power. Political institutions contribute to environmental problems because they are concerned with the distribution of resources and other benefits to society members.

In capitalist systems, political decisions are influenced by interest groups, one of the most powerful of which is corporations. Corporations are active in keeping environmental legislation at a minimum so that regulations will not be so stringent as to affect their profits seriously. Corporate managers frequently claim that environmental regulations reduce profits to the point that many companies, in order to comply, must either close down or drastically reduce the number of workers. Thus, corporate managers contend that, in the quest for environmental protection and preservation, jobs are inevitably lost. They argue that it is not possible for both the economy and the environment to be healthy.

When the environmental costs of production are externalized, do they fall equally on society's members? They do not if the system is stratified. *Social stratification* refers to the structured ranking of individuals and groups into horizontal layers according to important social markers—their possession of material objects or social attributes that are scarce in society and therefore highly prized. In a stratified social system, the higher social classes are more likely to reap the benefits from economic growth, while the lower social classes and the poor are more likely to experience the costs of economic growth through pollution in their communities and workplaces.

Through environmental threats, the poor have always disproportionately suffered the brunt of economic growth, but the nature and magnitude of those threats have changed throughout history. In the earliest days of urbanization, people moved from rural regions to larger villages and towns. Because space is a scarce resource in towns, allocated according to social class, the poor had to settle in the neighborhoods with the highest population densities. Such concentration exacerbated humankind's chronic maladies and, in the process, ironically revealed their environmental origin.

High population density, combined with the lack of sewage treatment and garbage removal, which is also typical to poverty, produced unsanitary conditions in the environment, resulting in a drastically increased susceptibility to contagious diseases. Sewage was thrown from residences directly into the streets. Garbage rotted on sidewalks or was carried off by packs of wild dogs. Contaminated water supplies gave rise to cholera epidemics, in which victims suffered from severe, watery diarrhea leading to rapid dehydration and death. Four cholera epidemics—in 1832, 1850, 1866, and 1873—left thousands dead throughout the United States. Smallpox and diphtheria were common. Typhoid fever struck victims in rapid succession, with severe headaches, fever, diarrhea, loss of appetite, and delirium. Infants died from the dehydration caused by rampant diarrhea. Flea-infested rats spread bubonic plague. During this period environmental threats were generated by natural processes, manifested in obvious conditions, and resulted in quick deaths. Indeed, it can be confidently stated that the greatest improvements in the history of public health derived not from the laboratory or the hospital but from systematic communal sanitation.

Population density became even greater with the Industrial Revolution. Portions of cities were entirely given over to industrial sites to support manufacturing processes. These areas were noisy, dirty, and sooty—undesirable locations for families. Consequently, it was less expensive to live in neighborhoods near the factories, slaughterhouses, and rail yards. It was the only housing the poor, who worked in these places, could afford.

Streets were covered with horse manure, which dried out and rose on the wind to form swirling dust clouds, which people inhaled. Large-scale burning of fossil fuels, the basis of the Industrial Revolution, blackened the air and generated lethal winter smogs. Respiratory diseases such as pneumonia, influenza, bronchitis, and tuberculosis became leading causes of death. Heart disease and cancers appeared more frequently. Thus, the environmental threats faced by the poor had changed with the Industrial Revolution: now threats were generated by industrial rather than natural processes. Nonetheless, they were still manifested in obviously deteriorating environmental conditions and relatively quick deaths.

The post–World War II period brought a significantly new kind of environmental threat. Since the war production processes have relied on the use of synthetic chemicals—manufactured substances that occur naturally nowhere on the earth. Many of these synthetic chemicals are harmful to organisms, a danger that is particularly great on farmlands that are sprayed with pesticides. In addition, the production of plastics releases synthetic chemicals into the air and water. Wastes containing chemical byproducts of manufacturing processes are buried in our soil and leak slowly into our groundwater supplies. And who lives and works in these areas? Mostly the poor.

The effects of some chemicals on human health are severe. For example, pesticides typically attack the nervous system. Rachel Carson in *Silent Spring* (1962) relates the experience of a chemist who, attempting to determine the toxic level of the pesticide parathion, swallowed a tiny amount, less than five thousandths of an ounce. "Paralysis followed so instantaneously that he could not reach the antidotes he had prepared at hand, and so he died" (Carson 1987:29). These new chemicals have been correlated with a list of ailments, including heart disease, birth defects, infant diseases, miscarriages, lung, breast and bone cancer, and leukemia.

This newest kind of environmental threat that disproportionately affects the poor is more insidious than past threats because, though generated by manufacturing processes, the effects are not always obvious. Nor is death so quick. The new environmental threats are often quite difficult to detect and their effects hard to prove. Cancers develop slowly over decades, and it is hard to show conclusively a causal link between illness and a substance in the environment. This very vagueness and uncertainty help to breed environmental conflicts and make it difficult to resolve them.

We have argued that the most powerful social groups in society have the most influence on decisions about environmental use. When economic growth rates are the basis of these decisions, the environment suffers. Therefore, an intimate and irrevocable relationship exists between economic development and the environmental degradation that disproportionately claims victims from the lower social classes. People at the top of a social hierarchy are seldom concerned with the interests of those at the bottom.

A POLITICAL ECONOMY PERSPECTIVE ON THE ENVIRONMENT

Environmental sociologists study how our beliefs, our social relationships, and the distribution of power in our society influence our decisions about environmental use. The particular paradigm to be used in this book to examine grassroots environmental conflicts is the political economy perspective, "a view of politics and power that recognizes the essential interweaving of state and economic institutions and the co-equal place of political and economic leaders in the power structure" (Marger 1987:5). Thus, the corporation and the state are the two key institutions of power in society. Power is an interplay of government and corporations. We emphasize these two institutions in analyzing environmental issues by first demonstrating their importance in examining the world.

Basic to an understanding of the world are issues regarding the state's role in society, which groups have the greatest influence in determining state policies, the causes and power of social movements, and the determinants of political behavior. The political economy perspective used in this book is based on three premises suggested by Szymanski (1978:1).

1. The source of political ideas and political behavior is contained in the experiences of people as structured by their economic position in society.

2. The state and state policies in the United States are dominated by the economic class that owns and controls the corporate economy.

3. The functions of the state in the United States are to stabilize society by securing the loyalty of the masses, to facilitate profit-making, and to increase economic productivity.

Many social analysts since Marx have supported his claim that the state plays a central role in society. The *state* is a social organization that exercises, within a given territory, an effective monopoly in the use of physical coercion. In the final analysis, the state rests on *force:* power whose basis is the threat or application of punishment. Although force is the ultimate basis of the state, it is seldom used; other, less blatant, forms of societal power are enough in most situations.

An important distinction must be made between the state and government. While the state is a social organization, *government* refers to the individuals and groups who control the state apparatus and direct state power. Government actually formulates the rules and policies that are authoritative, binding, and pervasive throughout a society. Government decisions affect the lives of all citizens through policies relating to environmental issues, the economy, military expenditures, education, and health care, among many others. Thus, politics is the process by which individuals and groups try to influence or control the policies and actions of governments at the local, state, national, and international levels. Political processes determine the distribution of goods and services—who gets what, when, and how. The procedures developed by a society to influence policy decisions regarding that distribution are collectively referred to as the political institution. Group influence on policy decisions varies with social class. A social class consists of all those individuals who share a similar relationship to property or the means of production. States are most acutely influenced by the economically dominant class.

A state does not rely exclusively on the use of physical force to maintain its hegemony; in fact, physical force is normally used only as a last resort. States normally guarantee the obedience of the majority through religion, nationalism, personal loyalties, voter apathy, and a common belief that the state operates in the interests of the society as a whole. The state actively promotes the idea that its domination is legitimate: that it is right that people follow its dictates because to do so is to follow God's will or the will of the people, or because the state has expert knowledge.

In the United States, a capitalist form of society, the state has three basic functions:

1. To preserve existing class relations by guaranteeing private property and law and order

2. To facilitate capital accumulation and profitability by regulating the labor force and the economy

3. To maintain the legitimacy of the state by protecting or appearing to protect all citizens.

Struggles within society over state policies are rooted in different material conditions of life. That is, political struggles are the manifestation of class struggles because the state operates primarily to benefit the upper classes. The interests of the upper classes are realized in the state through direct and indirect means.

One direct mechanism by which the upper class dominates the state is through the selection of candidates for top governmental offices. Except for representatives of popular movements in times of crisis, leading officials tend either to belong to the upper class, or to aspire to it and be willing to front for its interests in return for admission, or at least the trappings thereof. A second direct mechanism is through lobbying, in which business interests hire individuals to influence members of Congress and regulatory and administrative agencies.

Indirect control of the state by the upper classes occurs through three mechanisms (Szymanski 1978). First, capitalist values are propagated through socialization processes in the public education system, the military, the media, and religion. Second, if business interests are adversely affected by state policies, corporations can reduce production, relocate to other countries, or threaten either course of action. Both actions can generate an economic crisis for which the state would be blamed. Third, politicians who advocate anticapitalist policies face being cut off from the major source of campaign financing. Often the threat is enough to maintain the status quo, even if state officials themselves are not personally committed to capitalism.

The actions of corporate and government leaders have consequences for everyone, for these actions settle many important issues—jobs, prices, war or peace, and public services. Corporate leaders are largely unaccountable and seldom even identifiable to those outside the highest circles of power. Within government, decisions with societywide impact are increasingly made within the executive branch of the federal government rather than in the more broadly based Congress. With few exceptions, positions of power within the executive branch are not elective. Instead, they are appointive and therefore less sensitive to the constraints of public opinion. The increasing concentration of power within the economic and governmental realms has been accompanied by an increasing interaction between the two, and it is often difficult to separate them analytically. Their interests coincide, and they overlap in policy and personnel; they are mutually supportive.

How can we use a political economy approach to study grassroots environmental conflict? We will spend the rest of the book answering that question. We will analyze how economic decisions made by state and corporate leaders result in disruptions to ecosystems that differentially affect social classes. When affected social groups object to their exposure to environmental problems, conflict ensues. Grassroots environmental conflicts "are about the scarcity of ecosystem elements, as experienced by groups or social classes. They are thus struggles over decisions to allocate or restrict access by such classes or groups to ecosystems" (Schnaiberg 1980:3).

Political economy is a theoretical orientation to social structure and social change that examines economic class structures and their social consequences. According to Schnaiberg, "One crucial focus from political economy is its emphasis on sociopolitical legitimation and social control of economic and related activity. It seeks to trace the roots of both stability and change in sociopolitical conflicts. In the case of environmental conflicts, this seems especially appropriate" (1991:2).

We will illustrate the use of the political economy approach to grassroots environmental conflict with a hypothetical example. Let us say that a society is in the business of producing cherry pies as its economic base. State and corporate leaders decide together how big the pies will be, how the flour and other ingredients will be collected, what process will be used to bake the pie, how and where the cherry pits will be disposed, and how the finished pie will be divided among the citizens. But some citizens complain that they receive more pits than pies, while more fortunate citizens get more pies than pits. A conflict ensues. The corporation maintains that if they are forced to dispose of the cherry pits in another more expensive way, resulting in sky-high pie prices, they may instead shut down the ovens and put pie makers out of work. The state intervenes and tries to find a compromise, but is in the tenuous position of needing to support the profitable baking of pies to sustain the economy while protecting, or at least appearing to protect, the public from the hazards of cherry pits.

The production of goods and services in a society is similar to baking cherry pies. State and corporate leaders together decide what will be produced, how and from where the natural resources needed for production will be extracted, what production processes will be allowed, how wastes will be disposed, and how goods and services will be distributed throughout society. The inherent conflict of interests between citizens, unhappy about the distribution of environmental benefits and costs, and corporations, unhappy about the cost of meeting environmental standards, presents the state with the dilemma of choosing either to support the economy or to protect the public.

As we will see, the state has more often chosen to support the economy than to protect the public. The result is environmental problems. Before examining the social conditions that lead the state to make such a decision, we must gain a clearer understanding of the environmental impacts of economic growth and environmental degradation.

3. *And Industry Shall Inherit the Earth*

In this chapter, we demonstrate the link between economic growth and environmental problems in order to establish the foundation for our analysis of grassroots environmental conflicts. To see that critical link clearly, we should have an understanding of basic environmental science and industrial production processes.

AN ENVIRONMENTAL SCIENCE PRIMER

Environmental degradation is the disruption of the environment with negative consequences for ecosystems. The process of environmental degradation involves both *withdrawals* and *additions* to the environment (Schnaiberg 1980). Environmental withdrawals occur when something is removed from the environment, thereby consuming or destroying a resource, as in the extraction of coal or timber. Environmental additions occur when something is put into the environment that causes a detrimental change in the physical, chemical, or biological characteristics of the air, water, or soil and affects living organisms. To understand these processes, we need a basic understanding of environmental science.

Environmental science is that branch of physical science that is concerned with environmental issues. It is the study of ecological principles and their application to the human situation. Poor environmental planning is seldom due to the lack of ecological information; it is due primarily to the lack of its proper application. The objective of environmental science is to determine the conditions supporting a sustainable world, a world in which human populations can continue to exist indefinitely with a reasonably high standard of living and health.

Natural Resources

Natural resources are materials produced naturally in the physical environment, which are used to meet human needs. Examples are fertile soil, fresh water, fuel, building materials, fibers to make clothes, and physical space. Types of resources include soil; water; land; animals; plants; minerals; and energy.

Soil is a complex mixture of inorganic minerals (clay, silt, sand), decaying organic matter, water, air, and living organisms. Soil provides the nutrients for plants, and plants in turn, directly or indirectly, provide the food we and other animals require and serve as the base for producing the natural fibers, lumber, and paper we use.

Water is our most abundant natural resource. Over 70 percent of the earth's surface is covered with water, but only about 0.5 percent of it is available as fresh water. Yet fresh water is the substance most essential to life. A person can survive without food for about six weeks, but without water for only a few days.

Land resources include wilderness, forests, and rangelands. One reason why wilderness preservation is important is that it provides our only chance to study an ecosystem in its original complexity. Such studies often yield critical new forest products and biological methods of controlling pests. Forests provide wood for fuel, construction, and wood pulp. They also influence climate, add oxygen to the atmosphere, regulate water flow, provide habitats for organisms, cool and humidify the air, and absorb noise and some air pollutants. Rangelands are areas on which the vegetation is predominantly grasses. Cattle, sheep, and goats thrive on this vegetation and produce meat, milk, butter, and cheese for human consumption and nonedible goods such as wool and leather.

Animal and plant resources maintain the health and integrity of the world's ecosystems through the provision of food, the production and maintenance of oxygen, the decomposition of wastes, the recycling of nutrients, and the filtration and detoxification of poisonous substances. They also provide the sources for many foods, scents, soaps, dyes, natural insecticides, furs, natural rubber, and medicines.

Mineral resources are chemical elements or compounds, usually in solid form, that occur naturally in the earth's crust. They were produced through geochemical processes occurring over hundreds of millions of years during the earth's early history. Mineral resources are classified as metallic, such as iron, aluminum, copper, and tin, and nonmetallic, such as sand and salt.

Among our most important natural resources are those from which we obtain energy. For over 10,000 years, the main sources of energy for people were wood, sunlight, streams of water, and the muscle power of humans and draft animals. For billions of people today who still live in agrarian societies, the primary energy sources are the same. But, for those who live in industrial societies such as the United States, the main source of energy is *fossil fuels:* coal, natural gas, and petroleum. These fuels consist of the remains of ancient animals and plants, fossilized and compressed by geological processes in the earth's crust.

Resources may be classified as perpetual, renewable, or nonrenewable. A *perpetual resource* comes from what is essentially an inexhaustible source. Perpetual resources remain available in a relatively constant supply regardless of whether or how we use them. Examples are solar energy, winds, tides, and flowing water.

A *renewable resource* can be depleted in the short run if it is used or contaminated too rapidly, but normally it can be replaced in the long run through natural processes. Renewable resources include fertile soil, forests, animal and plant resources, and surface and groundwater.

Nonrenewable resources exist on earth in fixed amounts. They are either not replenished by natural processes, as is the case with copper, or they are replenished much more slowly than they are used, such as oil. Wilderness and rangeland resources, minerals, and fossil fuels are nonrenewable. A nonrenewable resource is considered depleted when 80 percent of its total estimated supply has been removed and used. To find, extract, and process the remaining 20 percent would cost more than it is worth. Only a few nonrenewable resources such as aluminum can be recycled or reused to stretch supplies.

Natural resources use is related to population size in that an increasing population causes a corresponding rise in use. In addition, a rise in the standard of living requires a rise in the average use of resources per person. Thus, resources are depleted in two general methods: by increasing population and by increasing standards of living. Natural resources are only one part of the earth's life support system.

The Earth's Life Support System

All forms of life depend for their existence on materials that compose four physical systems: the lithosphere, the atmosphere, the hydrosphere, and the biosphere.

The *lithosphere* is solid material; it is the upper surface or crust of the earth that contains soil, land, minerals, and energy resources. In contrast, the *atmosphere* is gaseous; it is the air we breathe, and it extends above the earth's surface. The *hydrosphere* refers to all of the earth's moisture—all of our water resources—in the forms of liquid, ice, and water vapor. The *biosphere* consists of those parts of the lithosphere, atmosphere, and hydrosphere which contain or support living organisms. The biosphere contains all plant and animal resources, and all the water, minerals, oxygen, nitrogen, phosphorus, and other nutrients that living things need.

To comprehend the fragility of the biosphere, imagine this: If the earth were an apple, the biosphere would exist within the apple *skin!* And everything in the apple skin is interdependent. If you disrupt one part of it, unintended and unpredictable consequences may appear in another part. If you release chlorofluorocarbons in North America, you get a hole in the ozone layer over Antarctica. Change one ecosystem, and you generate unpredictable changes in other ecosystems.

Ecosystems are the functional units of the biosphere in the same way that cells are the functional units of living organisms. An *ecosystem* contains all the populations of plant and animal species that live and interact in a given area at a particular time, as well as the chemical and physical factors that make up the nonliving environment. An ecosystem may be an ocean, a tropical rainforest, a fallen log, or a puddle of water. All of the earth's ecosystems put together make up the biosphere.

Life continues in an ecosystem unless conditions exceed the carrying capacity of the ecosystem. *Carrying capacity* refers to the maximum population of a given animal—including people—that an ecosystem can support without being degraded or destroyed in the long run. The carrying capacity can be exceeded, but not without lessening the system's long-term ability to support life.

Life on earth depends on two fundamental processes that operate through the components of an ecosystem. The first process is matter cycling, in which all matter is cycled through the components of the ecosystem in varying forms. The second is the one-way flow of high-quality energy from the sun in which solar energy enters the ecosystem as sunlight, is converted from one form of energy to another by the ecosystem's components, and then exits the ecosystem as heat. Different ecosystems support different types of plant and animal organisms that depend on the fundamental processes of matter cycling and solar energy flow.

The four components of an ecosystem are producers, consumers, detritus feeders, and decomposers. All four exist in each ecosystem. *Producers* are plants, such as trees, that manufacture their own food through photosynthetic processes. *Consumers* are organisms that feed directly or indirectly on producers; consumers are animals, including herbivores, carnivores, and omnivores—and people. *Detritus feeders* are organisms that consume dead plant and animal matter directly; some examples are vultures, earthworms, and termites. *Decomposers* are organisms whose feeding activity decays dead plant and animal matter.

Nature's delicate and ingenious balance can be seen in the way the inputs and outputs of producers, consumers, detritus feeders, and decomposers fit together perfectly in a natural recycling system. Plants produce organic material and oxygen that are needed by consumers for eating and breathing. The wastes from consumers are carbon dioxide and minerals, which are the nutrients that plant producers need. This is matter cycling and illustrates the first of three basic principles of ecosystem function.

Resources are supplied and wastes are disposed of by recycling all elements.

The second basic principle of ecosystem function concerns energy and states that

Ecosystems run on solar energy, which is exceedingly abundant, nonpolluting, relatively constant, and relatively everlasting.

Ecosystems convert energy from one form to another. For example, energy from sunlight is converted by photosynthetic plants to stored chemical energy, and the chemical energy is reconverted to various forms through food chains. At each step, a portion of the chemical energy (food) is broken down to release its potential energy. This energy is used by the organism to perform its work and is gradually converted to and lost as heat. Thus, energy enters ecosystems as light, performs work, and then exits as heat in a one-way flow of solar energy through the components of the ecosystem.

The third basic principle of ecosystem function is:

Large biomasses cannot be supported at the ends of long food chains.

As the population of a species within an ecosystem increases, organisms are forced to move down the food chain to survive, closer to the source of production. As each organism in the growing population eats, the mass of biological material in the ecosystem is reduced by the proportion represented by the food eaten by the organisms. The larger the number of ecosystems that are strained by growing populations, the greater the reduction of the total biological material in the biosphere.

These ecological principles carry important implications for humans. The first principle states that natural ecosystems gain resources and dispose of wastes by recycling all elements. Yet we humans operate in the ecosystem as if we could create elements at one point and make them disappear at another. This results in an unsustainable society, which cannot go on in this way indefinitely.

The second principle is that natural ecosystems sustain themselves by running on solar energy and could continue to do so virtually forever. People, in contrast, have thus far sustained societies by using fossil fuels, which are nonrenewable. Even though we have done so for only about 250 years, fossil fuels are already on the verge of depletion. Without an alternative source, energy resources will become more and more scarce, standards of living will fall, and the potential for conflict over dwindling fossil fuels will loom larger. As if that were not bad enough, the burning of fossil fuels is causing serious pollution problems, such as acid rain and the greenhouse effect.

The third principle is that large biomasses cannot be supported at the ends of long food chains. Implications for the earth's huge meat-eating population are profound. Raising animals for food requires much more fossil fuel energy than the animals themselves provide as food calories and protein. Since ten to twenty pounds of edible grains are consumed in producing one pound of meat, meat-eaters place an additional burden on agriculture, causing the destruction of land by both erosion and overgrazing.

Environmental problems are the result of people violating these three fundamental principles. Human intervention in the environment typically simplifies ecosystems, causing some species to exceed their limits of tolerance, which leads to environmental stress that can end in ecosystem collapse. What effects does the simplification of ecosystems return to people? What specific dangers do we face if we do not clean up our act? Schnaiberg distinguishes between two types of threats that such ecological disruption can generate for humans: direct biological threats to humans and threats to economic production (1980:28–38).

The biological threats that directly affect the survival of individual human beings include the spread of carcinogens and environmental toxins; the disorganization of the food systems necessary for present and future generations of people; and climatic changes that destroy habitats for humans. As living conditions deteriorate, leaving fewer and fewer favorable environments for human survival, conflict is inevitable.

With regard to the second type of threat, the threat to continuing economic production, simplification reduces our store of natural resources, which forms the absolutely required physical base for producing anything. Declines in economic production bring serious social problems for people, especially soaring unemployment rates, drastically reduced income, and government revenues insufficient to support public services and important social programs. Historically, such social problems have usually led to social conflict.

THE FRAGILE APPLE

The earth's life support system is quite fragile. Humans share the life support system of nature with other species. Even though they are often understood separately, all human economic, technical, political, and cultural activities are in fact ultimately rooted in and dependent on resources of the planet's biophysical environment.

Everything in the apple skin is interdependent. The relationships between living things and the earth form complex and delicately balanced webs of energy transformations and food chains. As cells are the functional units of organisms, so ecosystems are the functional units of the biosphere.

When, in the interests of economic development, we withdraw resources from the environment and introduce wastes back into it without concern for the environmental consequences, we violate ecological principles. Violation depletes resources and pollutes the earth. The survival of all living things depends on the earth's carrying capacity to support life. Environmental withdrawals and additions for the purposes of economic production tamper with the earth's carrying capacity. Thus, we endanger the fragile balance of the earth's life support system.

Finally, if we make decisions that give economic production priority over environmental protection, we can be assured that the earth will survive in some form—but, just as surely, life as we know it will *not*. We are all familiar with instances of unforeseen, unintended, and sometimes disastrous consequences of the most well-meant human interactions, from social programs to military intervention to trying to help a friend. Since the physical environment is more complex, much less well understood, and under more malevolent attack, such consequences are impossible to avoid. As Hoban and Brooks stated, "Pluck at any one point in the intricate fabric of our ecosystem and the web of relationships changes shape, disrupting the previous equilibrium so that further changes must be made to offset both intended and unintended effects" (1987:6).

We have provided this environmental science primer as preparation for the next section. A greater understanding of the workings of ecosystems permits a greater understanding of the mechanisms by which the expansion of industrial production affects ecosystems.

ECONOMIC GROWTH AND ENVIRONMENTAL DEGRADATION

Most nations in the world today are seeking to improve the quality of life through economic growth, which, as defined earlier, is an increase in the economy's capacity to provide goods and services for final use. Some debate the value of economic growth, but for many, a steady-state, no-growth economy is a frightening specter. Advocates for economic growth argue that growth is needed to maintain or to increase the standard of living, to provide jobs, and to accomplish such tasks as cleaning up pollution. They argue that without growth these circumstances cannot or will not happen.

Economic growth and development are supported in the United States because they create a larger stock of wealth to be distributed within the society. We return to our example of the production of cherry pies. If the number of cherry pies produced is constant, and particularly if the pies are not evenly distributed throughout society, conflict is inevitable. The lower classes clamor for a greater share of the pies, but for that to happen in a steady-state economy the upper classes must release some of their pies, which they do not want to do. Conflict is the consequence.

A solution that historically has made nearly everyone happy is economic growth: the production of more pies. Since the method of distribution remains the same, the increased production of cherry pies means that each social class receives the same *proportion* of the total number of pies produced as it did before, but the *actual amount* of pie each social class gets is increased. The historically neglected down side, of course, is that baking more pies requires more resources and more energy. That is, more flour, cherries, and energy must be withdrawn from the environment, and more cherry pits will be added to it. The inevitable consequence of producing more cherry pies, then, is a more degraded biosphere.

The biosphere—that thin "apple skin" which contains all of life—is a dynamic balancing act. Economic production by people, through withdrawals from and additions to the environment, brings both quantitative and qualitative disruptions to ecosystems. Increased volumes of production and increased byproducts of new technologies have generated modern pollutants. These new pollutants tend to have far longer transition times in the atmosphere and in the food chain.

A major kind of strain that people place on ecosystems comes from increases in economic growth. These increases translate to a higher standard of living for the society, which is manifested in the allocation of more units of resources per person. In industrialized nations such as the United States, increases in economic growth are accomplished in two ways: through agribusiness and through the expansion of industrial production. Both methods involve withdrawals from and additions to the environment that cause environmental problems. Our concern here is with the expansion of industrial production since it is most likely to lead to grassroots environmental conflict.

A Model of Industrial Production

The industrial production process begins with the extraction of raw materials—natural resources—from the lithosphere. This phase is typically called mining and has been at the center of a number of grassroots environmental conflicts. Once the raw materials have been mined, they are transported to a plant or factory where, in the next phase, workers transform the resources into manufactured products. In the final phase, manufacturing results in both a product to be sold to the public and a variety of wastes—materials that are unwanted byproducts of the processing phase. Frequently, grassroots environmental conflicts emerge over the disposal of these wastes.

Each *phase of the production process*—mining, transportation, manufacturing, and waste disposal—has three major effects on the environment.

First, each phase uses energy, contributing to the depletion of energy resources and to the pollution of the lithosphere, atmosphere, and hydrosphere in ways that adversely affect organisms in the biosphere.

Second, each phase depletes natural resources, making withdrawals from the environment which disrupt and simplify ecosystems and which reduce the stock of resources needed for further production.

Third, each phase pollutes the earth, making environmental additions to the lithosphere, atmosphere, hydrosphere, and biosphere that disturb the balance in ecosystems.

To help connect your understanding of environmental science to the emergence of grassroots environmental conflict, we next discuss each phase in the production process and its implications for environmental problems.

The Mining Phase of the Production Process

Both mineral resources and energy resources are mined. Both mineral resources and fossil fuels, our most used energy resource, are nonrenewable.

Use of a mineral resource involves several steps. First, a deposit containing enough of the desired mineral to make removing it profitable must be located. Second, some form of mining is used to extract the mineral from the deposit. Third, the desired form of the mineral is either used directly or manufactured into various products.

Once an economically acceptable mineral or energy deposit has been located, it is removed by surface or subsurface mining. Mineral deposits near the earth's surface are removed by surface mining in which mechanized equipment removes the overlying layer of soil and rock and vegetation so that the underlying mineral deposit can be extracted with large power shovels. Surface mining is used to extract about 90 percent of the metallic and nonmetallic minerals and almost two-thirds of the coal used in the United States. Almost half of the land disturbed by surface mining has been mined for coal.

When a mineral or coal deposit lies so deep in the ground that removing it by surface mining is too expensive, it is extracted by subsurface mining. In most subsurface mining techniques, a deep vertical shaft is dug and subsurface tunnels are blasted to get to the deposit. Then the mineral is hauled to the surface. Subsurface techniques are also necessary for extracting crude oil and natural gas. In one method, wells are drilled into underground rock reservoirs, allowing the pressurized oil or gas to rise to the surface. In a variation of that method, hot water is injected into the well to force the remaining oil to the surface.

Much of the equipment in mining procedures uses energy, primarily the burning of fossil fuels in the forms of oil or gas. Mining, then, contributes to air pollution by releasing substances that combine with sunlight to form photochemical smog. Mining also reduces the stocks of renewable resources such as plants (for example, tree harvesting for wood and paper products) and animals (for example, animal skins for tanning purposes).

The reserves of the nonrenewable resources extracted by mining are dwindling. According to the U.S. Bureau of Mines and the U.S. Geological Survey, the United States has adequate domestic reserves of most key minerals—except chromium, cobalt, platinum, tin, gold, and palladium—for at least the next several decades. But the Geological Survey estimates that present reserves of most key minerals will not satisfy U.S. needs for more than 100 years without increased recycling, conservation, and substitution.

More serious is the depletion of our fossil fuel reserves—the coal, oil, and natural gas on which industry currently depends. Coal is the most abundant fossil fuel. Identified coal reserves in the United States are projected to last about 300 years. Known reserves of natural gas in the United States are projected to last only until the mid- to late 1990s, while world reserves are expected to last until 2033. Most of the world's natural gas is located in the now-fragmented former Soviet Union. The world's oil reserves are primarily in the Middle East. According to estimates by the U.S. Department of Energy and the American Petroleum Institute, 80 percent of the world's known reserves of crude oil will be depleted by 2013. Even if more reserves are found, it would only postpone the inevitable; these resources clearly must be finite.

Mining procedures disturb ecosystems through pollution. Specifically, surface mining strips bare the land, destroying natural vegetation and habitats for many types of wildlife. If it is not restored, the exposed soil and mining wastes are subject to erosion by wind and water and can pollute the atmosphere and nearby water ecosystems. A serious problem in mining is the runoff of acids, silt, and toxic substances into nearby surface and groundwaters. Rainwater seeping through surface-mine spoils and through abandoned subsurface mines causes chemical reactions that produce sulfuric acid. Acid and other toxic compounds leached from mine spoils can run off into nearby rivers and streams, contaminating water supplies and killing aquatic life. Such pollutants can also percolate downward and contaminate groundwater.

In addition, the processing of extracted mineral deposits to remove impurities produces large quantities of rock and other waste materials called tailings, which are piled on the ground or dumped into ponds. Winds blow particles of dust and toxic metals from the piles of tailings into the atmosphere. Water leaches toxic substances into nearby surface water or groundwater supplies.

Most land disturbed by mining can be restored to some degree—although the preexisting ecosystem, in all its diversity, can never be artificially reproduced—and some forms of air and water pollution can be controlled. These efforts are expensive, however, and require energy that, in being produced and used, pollutes the environment. More than 1 million acres of American land disturbed by surface mining have long ago been abandoned by coal companies and not restored. Abandoned mines continue to cause serious environmental problems for those living nearby.

The Transportation Phase of the Production Process

In this next phase of the production process, natural resources are transported to the destination where they will be used, generally by truck or train. Transportation requires the use of energy, particularly the burning of fossil fuels. Similar to mining equipment's requirement of energy, transportation methods burn oil products that contribute to air pollution.

Motor vehicles produce carbon monoxide, nitrogen oxides, and photochemical pollutants. Carbon monoxide disrupts oxygen transport in the body; it is a serious health hazard. Large amounts of carbon monoxide cause death, as body tissues become starved for oxygen. At lower concentrations of carbon monoxide, more subtle human effects occur, such as decreases in ability to perceive the surroundings. Carbon monoxide has also been associated with some forms of heart disease, and it is a factor in heart attacks. Nitrogen oxides have been associated with respiratory diseases, heart disease, and cancer. Photochemical pollutants are associated with respiratory diseases and crop damage.

Air pollution is a kind of alphabet soup of chemicals and particulates. Photochemical smog is formed by a combination of primary and secondary pollutants that interact with sunlight. Smog is worst in urban areas where substances emitted from energy-burning vehicles mix with industrial air pollutants. And urban areas are generally the destination points for the delivery of natural resources for manufacturing.

The Manufacturing Phase of the Production Process

Manufacturing processes also use energy and so contribute both to the depletion of fossil fuels and to air pollution. The effects of burning fossil fuels that we discussed in regard to mining equipment and to transportation of resources absolutely pale in comparison to those generated in manufacturing processes.

About two-thirds of the coal in the United States is burned to generate electricity, with most of it used for industrial purposes. Coal produces more carbon dioxide when it is burned than does oil or natural gas. Carbon dioxide contributes to the greenhouse effect. Burning coal also produces particulate matter (mostly a fine dust known as fly ash), sulfur and nitrogen oxides that contribute to acid rain, several cancer-causing substances, and small amounts of radioactive materials naturally found in coal deposits.

Sulfur oxides and particulates injure plants, materials, and people. Leaves, needles, and plant tissues become bleached, and vegetation may die out completely. Carbonate building materials, such as marble and mortar, and metals, such as steel, copper, and aluminum, are corroded. Common cloth fabrics are damaged as well. Elevated levels of sulfur oxide and particulates have been linked to human illnesses and to deaths, particularly from respiratory illnesses. Sulfur oxide and particulates may also be *co-carcinogens*—substances that do not, by themselves, cause cancer but that can cause cancer in combination with some other substance.

Nitrogen oxides have direct effects on human health and plant life; nitric oxide (NO), an effective defoliant, was used extensively in Vietnam. But nitrogen oxides are most noted for their interaction with hydrocarbons in producing ozone. Necessary in the upper atmosphere but a harmful irritant at ground level, ozone aggravates diseases of the respiratory tract. Coal also contains arsenic in small quantities. Arsenic, a carcinogen, is released in fly ash or particulate matter when coal is burned. In addition, radioactive elements and their decay products are found naturally in fly ash.

The presence of sulfur oxides and nitrogen oxides in the atmosphere results in acid rain—that is, rain that is highly acidic. The chemicals fall or are washed out of the atmosphere and deposited on downwind land and bodies of water in rain, snow, sleet, fog, and dew. Acid rain reduces aquatic life, leaches important nutrients from the soil, damages trees and crops, and can adversely affect human life.

Some of the most dangerous substances in the smoke from burning coal are removed by devices that cause problems of their own. For instance, fly ash contains toxic substances. If it is captured by pollution control devices, it becomes a solid waste that must then be disposed of in landfills. Although sulfur dioxide can be removed from the coal smoke by pollution control devices known as scrubbers, scrubbers themselves produce a toxic waste containing fly ash and sulfur that must also be disposed of in a way that does not pollute water supplies and soil.

Burning fossil fuels during the manufacturing phase can also result in the thermal pollution of water. Electrical generators produce heat as waste that is typically dissipated by circulating water from lakes and rivers through the cooling systems, which is then returned to the waterway. Elevated water temperatures increase organic growth, overloading the system's decomposing and recycling mechanisms. The decomposition process consumes more oxygen, endangering those species of aquatic life which require the most oxygen. Thus a major effect of adding heat to aquatic ecosystems is the overall reduction of species, despite the many individuals of the surviving species.

The Waste Disposal Phase of the Production Process

Besides consumer items for the marketplace, manufacturing also produces waste. Since no production technology is waste-free, there is a continuous stream of waste emanating from every production process in the country, and so the problem of disposal arises.

Important distinctions need to be made between three types of waste: solid, hazardous, and toxic. *Solid waste* is the most inclusive term; it refers to any and all unwanted and discarded materials that are not liquids or gases. *Hazardous waste* refers to discarded materials in any form that could pose a serious threat to human health or to the environment. *Toxic chemical waste* constitutes a particular kind of hazardous waste that is widely produced in industry.

Most toxic chemicals belong to one of two classes: heavy metals or synthetic organic chemicals. *Heavy metals* are metallic elements that in pure form are heavy; that is, they have high atomic weights. Examples are lead, mercury, arsenic, cadmium, tin, chromium, zinc, and copper. Heavy metals are extremely toxic because, being soluble in water, they can be ingested and absorbed by organisms. In organisms, heavy metals tend to combine with and inhibit the functioning of particular enzymes. This effect can cause severe physiological or neurological consequences such as mental retardation, crippling, insanity, and birth defects.

Synthetic organic chemicals are human-made, carbon-based compounds that are the basis for all plastics, synthetic fibers, solvents, pesticides, and wood preservatives. Examples are dioxins, a group of about seventy-five different chlorinated hydrocarbon compounds, many of which are believed to be associated with liver cancer, birth defects, headaches, weight loss, hair loss, insomnia, and nerve damage; and polychlorinated biphenyls (PCBs), about seventy different benzene derivatives that until recently were used in electrical transformers and are associated with liver and kidney damage, gastric disorders, reproductive disorders, skin lesions, and tumors. Many synthetic organic chemicals are highly toxic because they are easily absorbed by the body but are nonbiodegradable. This means that the organism cannot metabolize the chemicals to remove them from the body and instead stores them in the body. The consequence of relatively high doses of synthetic organic chemicals can be acute poisoning or death. Even low doses over extended periods of time can be quite harmful by causing cancer, birth defects, liver and kidney dysfunction, or sterility.

Of the nearly 70,000 different chemicals in commercial use today, only about 20 percent have been extensively tested for toxicity, and some have not been tested at all. If all were tested, how many would be classified as hazardous?

Heavy metals and synthetic organic chemicals are insidious to organisms because they tend to bioaccumulate. *Bioaccumulation* means that small, seemingly harmless doses received over a long period of time accumulate in the body until they reach toxic levels and cause harm. Bioaccumulation occurs because the chemicals are nonbiodegradable and because they are excreted from the body only very slowly, if at all. In effect, the body acts as a filter, removing and accumulating these chemicals from all the food or liquids that pass through.

Bioaccumulation is compounded in a food chain. Organisms at the bottom of the food chain absorb the chemical from the environment and accumulate it in their tissues; in feeding on these organisms, animals at the next level up the food chain receive a higher dose and accumulate still higher concentrations in their tissues; and so on. Organisms at the top of the food chain, such as people, may accumulate levels that are as much as 100,000 times higher than environmental concentrations. Such concentrations are likely to have deadly effects. This concentrating effect that occurs through a food chain is called *biomagnification*. One of the more frightening aspects of bioaccumulation and biomagnification is that no signs of the processes occur until a dangerous level is reached. By then, it may be too late to do anything about it.

Further complicating the situation is the problem of synergistic effects. A *synergistic effect* occurs as a result of the interaction of two or more substances or factors that cause a net effect greater than that expected from adding together their independent effects. That is, the total effect of the interaction of the substances is greater than the sum of the two effects taken independently. Toxic chemicals seldom appear singly, and often a dozen or more occur simultaneously. An almost infinite number of combinations and relative concentrations are possible from a small number of chemicals, making the prediction of the synergistic effects of the wastes from even one process extremely difficult. If several manufacturers use the same ecosystem for waste disposal, prediction is virtually impossible, even if they freely disclose the nature of their waste. No one knows what will come out of such interactions.

We will use the term *toxic industrial wastes* to refer to toxic chemicals generated in production processes and discarded as waste. Toxic industrial wastes must be returned or added to the biosphere. They are placed, with varying degrees of care, in our air, water, and land, often contaminating those resources and leading to human illnesses and to the extinction of some species. It is this phase of the production process, the disposal of toxic industrial wastes, more than any other phase, that underlies grassroots environmental conflicts.

Whereas many of our toxic industrial wastes are produced by modern, high-technology methods, they are disposed of by methods so low-tech that they can only be called primitive. Historically, corporations have disposed of industrial wastes as expediently as possible. For example, the common practice in the past was to exhaust all combustion fumes up smoke stacks and to vent all evaporating materials into the air. All waste liquids and wash water contaminated with all kinds of materials were flushed into sewer systems or dumped directly into natural waterways. Many human health problems occurred, but they were either not recognized at the time as being caused by the pollution or were simply accepted as the price of progress. Much of our present understanding regarding the human health effects of these materials is derived from precisely these uncontrolled exposures.

As industrial production expanded and synthetic organic chemicals came into widespread use following World War II, many streams and rivers became essentially open chemical sewers. Not only were they devoid of life, but they were also hazardous. For example, in 1969 the Cuyahoga River flowing through Cleveland, Ohio, carried so much flammable material that it actually caught fire and destroyed seven bridges before it burned out. Public outcry over such incidents prompted Congress to pass the Clean Air Act of 1970 and the Clean Water Act of 1972.

Between 1950 and 1975, about 6 billion tons of industrial wastes were deposited on or under land throughout the United States. Industrial wastes were dumped in at least 26,000 sites before the present laws regulating disposal of such materials were enacted in 1976. The full extent of the problem is unknown because no one knows where all the dump sites are or exactly what is in them.

Currently, the Environmental Protection Agency's National Priority List for the cleanup of dump sites names over 900 sites as posing the most serious threats to nearby populations. The EPA estimates that the list could soon grow to 2000. The less conservative estimate of the Office of Technology Assessment is closer to 10,000 contaminated sites. Each contaminated site on the EPA's map represents a community where people live, raise their families, and work.

Each year, about 265 million tons of industrial wastes are created, or about 2000 pounds for every U.S. resident. Almost all the waste is stored or treated on site by large companies—the chemical producers, the petroleum refineries, and the manufacturers. The rest is handled by commercial facilities that profit from handling the hazardous waste generated by others.

Three methods are commonly used for the land disposal of industrial wastes: deep well injection, surface impoundments, and landfills. First, deep well injection involves drilling a well into dry, porous material below the groundwater in the belief that wastes pumped into the well soak into the porous material and remain isolated from groundwater by impermeable layers. Second, in surface impoundment, waste is discharged into a sealed pit or pond so that solid wastes settle and accumulate while water evaporates. The idea is that, if the bottom is well sealed and evaporation is equal to input, surface impoundments can receive industrial wastes indefinitely. Third, when toxic industrial wastes are in a concentrated form, they are commonly put into drums and buried in landfills. If a landfill is properly lined, covered, and supplied with a means to remove material that leaks through, it is presumed to be safe.

Land disposal poses two serious problems. The first is ensuring that the industrial wastes actually arrive at the proper disposal facilities. When the Clean Water Act of 1972 restricted the flushing of chemical wastes into sewers or rivers, many companies were caught without alternative means of disposal. But, of course, the industrial wastes did not just disappear. Wastes that were no longer emitted into the air and discharged into the water were redirected toward land disposal. Because the potential shortcomings and dangers of this redirection were not adequately considered at the time, land disposal and the potential for groundwater pollution increased enormously.

As stacks of drums of hazardous wastes mysteriously began to appear in abandoned warehouses, vacant lots, or municipal landfills where such dumping is illegal, it became clear that some individuals were taking advantage of the situation. For a fee, these "toxic entrepreneurs" would dispose of a company's hazardous wastes. In case after case, they simply pocketed the money, leaving the toxic chemicals in any untended locations they could find, and disappeared without a trace. Thus, no one could be found who was legally responsible for the waste. This practice has been dubbed *midnight dumping*.

A second serious problem associated with land disposal is ensuring that the disposal facilities are properly constructed, managed, and sealed. During the late 1970s, it was discovered that many of the landfills, impoundments, and wells in which industrial wastes had been placed had pitifully few, if any, precautions to make them secure. Hundreds of abandoned dump sites across the country have been used for industrial wastes. Frequently, they are discovered only when residents of a community, on the basis of shared patterns of illnesses among families, begin to suspect something is wrong.

Prior to the late 1970s, very little attention was directed either to monitoring the amount and kinds of wastes being generated or to ascertaining where and how they were being disposed. Apparently, few really considered the possibility that disposing of wastes in the ground might endanger public health. In 1978, however, problems inherent in the land disposal of industrial wastes became evident.

The EPA now estimates that as recently as the late 1970s, 90 percent of our toxic industrial wastes were being disposed of improperly. Landfills had no liners or leachate collection systems. Some landfills were discovered in which wastes were actually immersed in groundwater. Surface impoundments did not have sealed bottoms, so percolation of the wastes was going directly into groundwater. Injection wells were found in which wastes were being deposited just above aquifers or even directly into them. Even in many new sites designated for wastes, the EPA found that monitoring systems were inadequate to detect leakage.

The World Resources Institute has estimated that as many as 75,000 active industrial landfill sites along with 180,000 surface impoundments and 200 other special facilities may be possible sources of groundwater contamination. The level of toxicity that constitutes danger to organisms—particularly humans—has become a highly controversial issue.

SUMMARY

Modern production and its technology have created enormous pollution problems, largely because the pollution costs are heavily borne by the larger society, including people who live near polluting facilities, instead of being included in the cost of production. When such costs are externalized, the marketplace loses any ability to perform a regulating function. Reform or external regulation are resisted because of the short-term profit orientation and the extremely individualistic and self-seeking values of the capitalistic system.

Defenders of the established ways of doing things argue that those who raise the issues of the social costs of economic growth are opposed to all growth and progress. Yet the real issue is not growth or no-growth but the character and quality of that growth and who determines its direction.

4. *Live Long and Prosper*

We said in Chapter 2 that the political economy perspective on environmental issues is an analytical view that recognizes the interweaving of state and economic institutions. In this perspective, the corporation and the state are the two key institutions of power in U.S. society. We have demonstrated that a major cause of environmental problems is economic growth, which takes place largely through the expansion of industrial production. Industrial production frequently generates grassroots environmental conflict because of disagreements about the environmental consequences of mining, transportation, manufacturing, and waste disposal to host communities. Thus, an understanding of this conflict requires an understanding of the roles of the corporation and the state in making decisions about whether to increase, maintain, or limit the rate of economic growth. If the two entities differ in their approach to economic growth, a stalemate in decision making is likely. If their views are similar, corporations and the state have a synergistic effect in setting economic and environmental agendas for the nation.

In this chapter, we examine the relationship between economic development and the state by discussing the functions of the state, the dimensions of corporate power and the growth coalition. We ask, Who will protect the environment from the consequences of industrial production? The state? Corporate America? The workers who actually carry out production activities?

THE FUNCTIONS OF THE MODERN CAPITALIST STATE

Three basic characteristics shape the production system and its complementary social institutions in modern capitalist society: private ownership of property, competitive pursuit of profit, and inequality in the distribution of social wealth. On all three counts, the U.S. socioeconomic system is fundamentally capitalist. The modern capitalist state influences all areas of life. It conducts relations with other states, establishes social policy, provides infrastructure services such as transportation and communications, directly produces goods and services for sale, intervenes in industrial relations, regulates business, and, since World War II, has assumed responsibility for overall economic management (Gough 1979).

Growth in the capitalist state's activities has increased substantially in the post–World War II era, which is frequently referred to as the advanced capitalism period. Prior to this era, under laissez-faire and then monopoly capitalism, the state played only a minimal role in the economy. Gradually, the capitalist state's role of creating the conditions for capitalist production expanded to include the abetting of the development of monopoly capital (Gough 1979).

In his important book *The Fiscal Crisis of the State* (1973), James O'Connor identifies two fundamental and sometimes contradictory functions of the modern advanced capitalist state: accumulation and legitimization. *Accumulation* refers to the state's obligation to create and maintain the conditions under which profitable capital accumulation is possible. The state's second function, *legitimization,* dictates that the state must also simultaneously create and maintain conditions of social harmony, which includes public protection. These role obligations of aiding economic growth while protecting the public frequently create a serious dilemma for the state: "A capitalist state that openly uses its coercive forces to help one [social] class accumulate capital *at the expense* of other classes loses its legitimacy and hence undermines the basis of its loyalty and support. But a state that ignores the *necessity of assisting the process of capital accumulation* risks drying up the source of its own power, the economy's surplus production capacity and the taxes drawn from this surplus" [italics added] (O'Connor 1973:6).

Other analysts make the same observation in somewhat different terms. For example, Shover, Clelland, and Lynxwiler (1986) base their analysis of federal regulation of the coal industry by the Office of Surface Mining on the premise that "the state is dependent on [economic] growth for its resources and legitimation" (1986:127). Similarly, in his work on theories of the state, Block observes that the state depends on a healthy economy in order to provide legitimacy for the regime and the tax revenues for financing state activities (1977).

All these analyses of the modern capitalist state eventually reached the same conclusion: the state's accumulation function is in contradiction to the legitimization function because the two functions serve different social class interests. Enhancing conditions for profitability directly serves the upper classes, the corporate classes, while maintaining social harmony and protecting the public most serve the interests of those without the power to adequately protect themselves, namely, the middle and working classes.

Moreover, protection is frequently most needed *from* the upper and corporate classes, resulting in direct conflict of state functions. Wherever the interests of the major social classes are at odds with one another, the state's functions are in contradiction. What are the consequences? Compromise is always possible, but Americans tend to view compromise as the failure of both sides. Generally, one of the major social classes will be neglected and will not have its interests adequately served by the state.

Accumulation

The U.S. system is often described as a mixed economy, denoting the participation of both public and private institutions in the economy. In reality, it is mixed only in the sense that government and private enterprise each participate in various ways to shape economic policy and stimulate a sound economic climate. Although in a few instances the state supplies services (for example, mail delivery and highways), the vast bulk of the U.S. economy is privately owned and controlled. In this regard, the country is unique even within the capitalist world. In almost all other modern capitalist societies, at least the basic industries are publicly owned. In Great Britain, for example, power companies, communications systems, railroads and airlines, coal mining, and steel production are primarily state, that is, public enterprises.

Profits are the motivational underpinning of capitalism. People in capitalist societies are expected to maximize their wealth by competing with one another in production. The society's wealth and the means by which it is produced are by and large private. As a result, the profits that are generated are private profits. Although pursuing self-interest is common in all societies, under capitalism it becomes a cultural value that is considered socially beneficial and morally correct. With such an emphasis on individualism, public needs are met only when meeting them has a minimal effect on private gain. The state will not compete with private industry. Even public programs such as health, education, and housing are dependent on private firms for materials and services. As a consequence, not only private investment but also public investment results in private profits.

As a system founded on individualistic competition, capitalism inevitably results in inequalities in the distribution of wealth. Indeed, inequality is considered desirable, since it is inequality that makes competition meaningful. But an important distinction exists between accumulated wealth and the means for generating wealth: namely, accumulated wealth is the amount of money an individual controls in the form of cash, stocks, and bonds. Most people in capitalist societies own some private property— clothes, cars, household appliances, electronic equipment, and even their homes. However, these personal forms of ownership do not constitute wealth because they actually count for very little in the overall distribution of wealth in society.

The means for generating wealth refers to the amount of capitalist property an individual owns that can be used to generate further income and wealth. The critical forms of ownership are factories, machines, real estate, and financial capital because they constitute the means of production, the mechanisms through which industrial production occurs. Control of these mechanisms enables the conversion of industrial production into increasing amounts of income and wealth.

Wealth is the most essential source of political power because it is most easily transformed into authority and influence. Within a society, political power is more closely related to unequal distribution of capitalist property than to inequalities in accumulated wealth. In the United States and other capitalist societies, giant industrial and financial corporations possess the greatest capitalist property. The overriding characteristic of the U.S. economy today is the dominance of the corporation as the chief form of enterprise and the source of economic wealth in society. Thus, corporate owners and managers who control corporate wealth are the dominant influence on the state's economic policies. The state, seeking to better perform its accumulation function, actively solicits corporate input in policy-making. Corporate dominance in federal economic policy has developed in the past 100 years at the same time that the United States evolved into a major industrial power.

This modern form of capitalism, characterized by the concentration of wealth known as *corporate capitalism,* bears little resemblance to the market economy of 100 years ago. Although most of the more than 20 million businesses in the United States are small in size, in almost every area of economic activity power has been concentrated in a few hundred giant corporate enterprises (companies such as IBM, General Motors, Ford, Chrysler, General Electric, Hewlett-Packard, and Westinghouse). The free market forces that are so evident at the small business level operate inefficiently, if at all, in the presence of so much concentration of power.

Thus, under corporate capitalism, the society's productive resources are controlled by a relatively few large corporations and their itinerant executives who work in conjunction with provisional state officials to increase profitability and economic growth. The payoff of the partnership for the corporate class is a literal payoff—greater wealth. The payoff for the state is the successful performance of its accumulation function. What does this concentration of political and economic power mean for the average citizen? How does the power of the corporation affect society as a whole?

The corporate executive's most critical decision-making power is the power to decide where and when corporations will invest their resources and in what amounts. The corporate class possesses such great decision-making power because the system is founded on *private* ownership: whoever owns property, or manages it for the owners, has the right to make decisions about that property. Consequently, the number and types of jobs that are created and lost, and the location of plants and equipment that can make or break a local community's economy, are determined primarily by the corporate class in partnership with the state.

The crucial nature of corporate investment for local economic stability can be seen in the efforts of state and local governments to lure industries to their communities. Financial incentives, such as tax breaks and the use of public lands, are used to attract industry that will create local jobs and increase local revenues. Quite frequently, the inducement is environmental. A corporation considering the construction of a new steel mill in a poor, rural area may be promised a variance from environmental laws, that is, legal permission from the state to violate the laws. For example, the corporation might be permitted to overlook certain regulatory standards regarding their air emissions in exchange for locating in the community. Corporate executives seek such propositions because they increase short-term profits. For its part, the local government approves because these propositions have the short-term effect of saving a sagging local economy. These propositions are made so commonly and so widely that one could argue that the traditional lobbying process has been reversed: state and local governments are now the lobbyists, petitioning the powerful corporations.

A popular cultural myth is that an objective consumer market determines which goods are available for purchase and at what prices, but in truth, the needs of corporate enterprise determine the availability of goods and their prices. Our foods, our clothes, our cars, and our television programs represent the decisions of corporate executives, for corporate capitalism does not rely simply on *meeting* human needs but on *creating* them. A major tenet of corporate capitalism is that constant growth, through the development of new markets and the creation of demand for goods, is necessary to maximize profits. Because meeting only the existing demand for consumer products does not generate further growth, corporations continually stimulate demand by creating markets for their products through planned obsolescence, advertising, and expansion into foreign countries. Advertising, as the key mechanism in stimulating consumer demand, has become an article of faith, shaping American capitalism in its image. Corporations allocate billions of dollars annually to media advertising in the belief that it creates demand for products. Soap and detergent firms, for example, spend 20 percent of their annual sales revenues on advertising (Marger 1987).

The timing and rate of the introduction of technological changes in society are determined to a great measure by corporations. Since only corporations possess the economic resources to support substantial research and development programs, the corporation ultimately determines which technological advances will be developed into consumer products. As in other aspects of corporate enterprise, technological choices are made on the basis of short-term profit projections rather than societal needs. Values regarding private property embedded in our social institutions demand that the choices be made in this way. For example, whether the United States will rely in the future on oil, nuclear power, solar power, or some other form of energy is still undetermined. But as long as the development and production of energy remain dependent primarily on the private corporation and the costs of extraction, energy decisions will be made more on the basis of corporate needs—that is, profitability—than on long-range societal needs, such as resource conservation and environmental protection, which are rarely considered until they become crises.

Corporations exercise enormous power over public affairs while operating as private institutions. That is, even though corporate decisions carry consequences for the public at large, our social institutions and our cultural system dictate that corporate decisions stay in the private hands of the corporate executives. For example, a paper mill in Virginia may decide to relocate in Mexico rather than renovate the mill to comply with environmental laws. The decision is dictated by the executives' plans for advancement, based on the realization of the corporation's explicit charge to maximize profits for shareholders. This privately made decision affects the public at large because the mill's relocation also relocates jobs and destroys the community's economic base. Or the paper mill may be granted a variance from environmental laws so that it stays in the community. Jobs are protected, but the public at large is adversely affected by deteriorating environmental quality.

Giant corporations have greater social and economic influence than does any other social institution—often even greater than the state itself. Investment, jobs, education, material goods, technological change, and the mass media are all significantly influenced by corporate executives. And yet this group, the corporate class, remains largely inaccessible, unaccountable, and unknown to the general public, semi-hidden behind the state as the state seeks to fulfill its accumulation function.

Legitimization

In its legitimization role, the state is required to provide protection to the public at large, including protection from the negative consequences of corporate decisions. Thus, besides its booster role that emphasizes accumulation, the state must also play a regulatory role in relation to the corporate class. The possible contradiction in state functions becomes apparent: through its accumulation function the state aids corporations, while through its legitimization function it restrains corporations.

One basic form of state intrusion into the economy is the establishment of regulatory agencies to control the social costs of production. Beginning with the Interstate Commerce Commission established in 1887, government agencies have routinely been created by Congress to regulate society's commercial life. Industries that do not come under the purview of a specific regulatory body are covered by generic agencies such as the Federal Trade Commission. Virtually every business activity is linked to the government through regulatory agencies, which then, in theory, have the potential to play a powerful controlling role over corporations.

To the extent that regulatory agencies do not exercise such control, we can infer influence by members of the corporate class. This influence has been so extensive and so effective that today regulatory agencies are composed of representatives of and aspirants to the very industries the agencies are charged with overseeing. Regulatory agencies operate more often as corporate than as public agents, formulating and enforcing policies that actually promote and protect the supposedly regulated industry.

The Corporations' broad influence in government regulatory agencies is not recent. Gabriel Kolko (1967) found that, during the Progressive era of the early twentieth century, the formation of regulatory bodies, which were ostensibly designed to establish public control over the increasing power of the corporate class, was not really a victory for the anti-business forces but was a triumph for the corporations themselves. Corporations, in fact, led the struggle for the federal regulation of the economy by lobbying Congress to restrict unfair business practices. From the very beginning of government regulation of business, therefore, corporate executives have played leading roles in the regulatory agencies.

Consequently, regulatory measures were not a threat to the corporate class. The corporate elites viewed the agencies as mechanisms they could use to restrain unfair business practices; control or eliminate competition, giving corporations a measure of security they would long deny to labor; create a favorable environment for continued expansion; and, by cooperating in the formation of the agencies, influence future government regulatory policies. Through state intervention in the form of regulatory agencies, corporations received several significant benefits: protection from foreign competition by the imposition of tariffs; grants to land and other natural resources; access to state coercion against striking workers; and exemptions from tax payments. Regulatory agencies also erected a barrier between corporations and complaints by the public and provided protection against legislation that was hostile to corporate interests.

Thus, through the influence of the corporate class, government regulation itself has contributed to the growth, concentration, and noncompetitive nature of today's economic system. Regulatory agency personnel still tend to come from corporate backgrounds; the phenomenon has been called the revolving door syndrome. Regulatory administrators are familiar with the industries they regulate because they have frequently held managerial positions in them prior to government service. Furthermore, the government regulators often return to the industries after they leave the agencies. Many people question whether such persons can impartially represent the public one day, knowing the potential rewards available from the corporate class the next.

Besides the revolving door syndrome, another factor contributes to the regulatory agencies' lack of control over corporations. Regulatory agencies typically lack the financial and personnel resources to challenge corporate practices. The Food and Drug Administration (FDA) is an example. The FDA is charged with assuring the quality of all food, drugs, and cosmetics sold in the nation. This function entails the regulation of the manufacture and sales of drugs made by about 3500 companies, and all foods consumed in the United States, involving 30,000 production and processing plants and 40,000 packing and storing facilities. To monitor such vast industries, the agency employs only about 8500 people and operates on an annual budget of about $300 million. As a result, the FDA is forced to rely primarily on the food and drug companies themselves to supply the agency with information on procedures and new products. In effect, then, food and drug companies regulate themselves. This pattern of self-enforcement is repeated in each of the regulated industries.

Regulation is the outcome of social conflict, the political resolution of social struggle. It is a political process, and political conflicts are never fully resolved. While government regulation theoretically controls powerful economic institutions and forces them to act in the public interest, the fact is that they most often fail to regulate effectively. Such is the case with the Environmental Protection Agency (EPA).

The EPA's regulation of corporate activities involves government intervention in the economy to establish parameters for environmental withdrawals and additions by the nation's production processes. *Environmental regulation* is "a calculated intrusion by the state into the workings of the economy" (Shover, Clelland, and Lynxwiler 1986:x). Since the market cannot regulate environmental practices unless they are reflected in the prices of specific products made by specific manufacturers—that is, unless the environmental costs of production are not externalized—the government intervenes to specify through laws what may and may not be done. If regulations are enforced equally, they are outside market forces, and they actually permit environmentally concerned industries to follow their consciences without suffering economically. However, if they are not enforced equally—because of local variances, relocation abroad, corruption—again, as a significant cost of production, they come under the sway of the market.

But environmental laws only represent the government's intent to regulate economic behavior by corporations. The laws themselves have only symbolic value unless they are "backed by the mobilization of state power which entails enforcement (mobilization of a state administrative apparatus) and sanctions (mobilization of a state judicial apparatus). Behind these are the state's legal monopoly on the use of force (the state's repressive apparatus)" (Shover, Clelland, and Lynxwiler 1986:1).

Law enforcement and regulatory officials represent the state, and the state, as we discussed earlier, is charged with the contradictory functions of facilitating the objectives of corporations (the corporate class) while providing for the public welfare (the middle and working classes). This dilemma may be regarded as a manifestation of the inherent contradictions between liberal and democratic principles (Habermas 1975; O'Connor 1973; Wolfe 1977).

We use the term *liberal* in the historic rather than the contemporary sense of the word. Liberalism developed in the eighteenth and nineteenth centuries as a movement for individual liberty in the political, economic, and religious realms of life. It is an ideological orientation based on a belief in the importance of the freedom of the individual. In the economic realm, liberalism supported free competition and opposed all but the most essential governmental interference in economic activities (Theodorson and Theodorson 1969:230).

Since liberal ideology demands that responsibility for economic decisions be placed in the hands of the owners of private property, the state should interfere only to promote capital accumulation. At the same time, the state must maintain its legitimacy through popular support, and, according to democratic ideology, decisions affecting the majority must be made by the majority. Herein lies the contradiction: economic decisions that have consequences for the public are made without input from the public. Such a course is consistent with liberal ideology but in clear violation of democratic ideology. As Wolfe states, "The predicament of a liberal democracy is that liberalism denies the logic of democracy and democracy denies the logic of liberalism, but neither can exist without the other" (1977:7).

The tensions that arise because of the different expectations deriving from liberal ideology and democratic ideology periodically generate crises for the state. These crises affect either the state's accumulation function, in which case corporations demand state intervention to promote policies of economic growth, or the state's legitimacy function, in which case the public demands democratic change. Historically, in its response to these crises, the state has tended to lean toward continuing capital accumulation and economic growth and to make the minimum accedence to the majority necessary to satisfy legitimacy (Wolfe 1977).

The contradictory roles of the state are clearly manifested in the federal government's actions on environmental issues. To assure increasing economic growth, the state has consistently fostered the accumulation of capital by limiting corporate liabilities for environmental damages. As economic growth and capital accumulation increase, however, resource depletion and pollution also increase. The costs are then borne by the public, who must pay either in polluted environment or in the taxes necessary to clean it up. By promoting legislation that permits corporations to externalize the environmental costs of production, the state fails to provide for the public welfare and thereby endangers its legitimacy. When people revoke their approval of the government because of its inability to deal effectively with environmental problems, the result, more and more frequently, is grassroots environmental conflict.

Despite the risk of losing its legitimacy, the state most often comes down on the side of capital. In order to understand what appears to be government's willful neglect of duty, let us examine closely the power of the corporate class and its ties with the state.

THE DIMENSIONS OF CORPORATE POWER

In the United States, the state's first priority is to keep the economic system running smoothly and efficiently. As a result, the bulk of public policy decisions, even war and peace, concerns economic issues. Although the basis of state action is not always economic considerations, the structure within which the political system operates is essentially determined by the needs of the economic system. In such a structure of power, the corporate class and the state naturally interlock. The state tends to favor the interests of the corporate class when they are in conflict with those of other groups. In other words, economic power is transformed into political power.

The transformation of economic power into political power predates the emergence of the corporate class. "Business goals have been indigenous to our national development, as have the efforts of those with economic interests to implement such goals through political means" (Epstein 1969:21). The preeminence of business interests and business values— that is, those pertaining to the manufacture and exchange of goods for profit—has never been seriously challenged, and no other social institutions have ever played such a coordinate power role as business and the government in the United States.

During the past half century, the expanded role of government has paralleled the growth of the corporation. Indeed, the growth of one institution aided the growth of the other to such an extent that the two now maintain a symbiotic, mutually supportive relationship. In their current forms, it would not be possible for them to operate independently. The state's chief role in its symbiotic relationship with business is to maintain, support, and coordinate the corporate capitalist system and to assure a social climate favorable to growth and prosperity. The federal government, sometimes in cooperation with state and local governments, uses four key mechanisms to support the corporate system: the regulation of business by various governmental agencies; the provision of taxation and subsidies to the private sector; the consumption of goods and services; and the management of foreign policy (Marger 1987:127–138).

In its turn, government depends on corporations to assure the social and political stability that results from basic corporate decisions on economic growth, employment, and industrial output. Politicians must at least appear to deliver on economic issues or they will not be reelected, and government policy must reflect the general needs of the corporate system because of the corporate sector's control of the society's productive resources.

Thus, the state and the corporate class are integral parts of the capitalist socioeconomic order, bound together through the mutual and public-supported goal of the society's economic well-being. One need not see conspiracy among political and economic elites to recognize the mutuality of their interests. In a class-stratified society in which economic power is so highly concentrated, people at the top of the stratification system who own or control the society's wealth hold a tremendous advantage over others in gaining access to the state and making it work in their interests. With virtually unimpeded access to government leaders through lobbying, campaign financing, and the interchange of personnel, corporations exert constant influence on the shaping of public policy. This concentration of power in a limited number of large corporations has resulted in a system in which the basic economic decisions of production and distribution, once made by the supply-and-demand dictates of the market, are now largely made by a corporate elite consisting of top-ranking corporate executives who control corporate wealth and make key corporate decisions.

Sociologist Harold R. Kerbo argues that the corporate elite constitutes an emergent corporate class that has replaced the old ruling class in the United States (1983). In earlier periods, the top of the old stratification system contained a group of families that dominated the country through their ownership and control of the most important sources of wealth—the means of production. The families extended their economic dominance into the political sphere through direct participation in government (for example, as appointees to the president's cabinet), selection of other major government officeholders (through campaign contributions), and extensive lobbying in Congress.

Today, Kerbo maintains, a corporate class, holding key positions of authority in major corporations, forms a network of associations, much like the old upper class families. These associations crisscross major corporate institutions, creating an interpersonal web of relations at the top of these institutions. These corporate executives constitute a social class because they have economic interests in common, possess enough unity and intraclass organization to recognize common class interests, and have the means to dominate the economy and political system. The corporate class retains many of the same characteristics as the old upper class. Unlike the old upper class, however, the basis of the corporate class's power is not *ownership* of the means of production but *control* of the major means of production, the big corporations. The corporate class is above the interests of separate, competing corporations. Rather, their interests lie in maintaining the structure of corporate capitalism, interests that unite the corporate class into a complex of interrelated corporate bodies. Since their most basic interests are the same, they have considerable motivation to restrict competition to nonlethal forms and marginal gains and losses.

Members of the corporate class are chief executive officers or board members of one major corporation, while simultaneously serving as board members in other corporations. They are quite familiar with the ways of government. Many, in fact, have moved in and out of government in various capacities, such as advisers, cabinet secretaries, or special committee members. They may change jobs, but their personal as well as class interests lie not just with one corporation but with the structure of corporate concentration as a whole. Members of the corporate class often belong to the same exclusive social clubs, maintain vacation residences in the same exotic locales, and send their children to the same exclusive private schools. Unlike the old upper class, however, they are transients with primarily short-term needs who have no permanent ties with one corporation, its workers, or the community in which it resides.

This view of the corporate class is not based on a conspiracy theory that sees evil forces or evil people at work in the world. Rather, in this view the corporate class is a *social structure* that provides a group of people with the power to protect and maintain their particular economic and political interests, even when these interests are in conflict with those of others in the society.

Thus, a relatively small number of corporate giants with various ties among themselves dominate the economy. Through economic domination, they have obtained tremendous political influence as well. The actions, or inactions, of the major corporations have serious consequences for millions of people. Our other social institutions, such as the family, education, the polity, and religion, cannot fully be understood in isolation from these powerful economic institutions.

THE GROWTH COALITION

We have said that, given the economic system, corporations *must* maintain profits through the economic exploitation of the environment because the structure of the economic institution compels them to do so. For example, imagine the case in which the CEO of a poodjet factory has an emotional and awakening confrontation with her 20-year-old offspring, who is taking an environmental sociology class. As a result, the CEO becomes urgently concerned about the environment, and she makes changes in the production process so that her factory does not pollute the environment.

But the change in poodjet technology is expensive in its development, implementation, and maintenance phases. These expenses are reflected in the price of the product, so that the poodjets from this factory cost significantly more than those produced at other factories. These more expensive poodjets are displayed in discount stores alongside poodjets of similar quality but lower cost. When consumers come in search of a poodjet, which one will they buy? The market behavior of consumers living near the plant may reflect their environmental concern (or it may not, if they depend on the factory for their livelihoods), but since these poodjets are sold nationally, most consumers have no idea of the *local* environmental problems this factory is trying to address. Consumers will likely make self-serving attributions about the higher prices—the owners are greedy or they are inefficient. Consumers may actually feel good about punishing our misunderstood, environmentally benign poodjeteers. In the end, they buy the cheaper poodjet.

Before long, the CEO is terminated by the board of directors, and her business career takes a severe turn for the worse. Without environmental regulations to force uniformity and protect her, the CEO, who was merely a manager and was prohibited the luxury of practicing altruism using other people's money, literally could not afford to protect the environment.

As we have seen, however, corporations are not alone. They operate in conjunction with the state to form a powerful force in promoting economic growth, even at the expense of the environment. One might expect resistance to the combined force of the state and the corporate class to come from labor. After all, the working class is more likely than higher social classes to bear the social costs of expanded industrial production in the form of environmental threats in the workplace and the community. Yet, historically the working class has joined forces with corporations and the state. What seems at first to be an unholy alliance turns out to be a rational choice for the working class, *given their structural position in society*. Since they must always be concerned for their short-term economic existence, they must also make short-term decisions. Consequently, corporations, the state, and the working class form a coalition in support of economic growth. Schnaiberg (1980) refers to these three groups as the *growth coalition*, a confederation of diverse groups with the same goal of economic growth. What social forces have historically compelled the working class to remain bound into the growth coalition?

The position of the working class, the standard of living, and the objective conditions of work have improved markedly since the degrading conditions typical of the late nineteenth century. These improvements are the results of various social forces and institutions, including the state's intervention in dealing with the boom-and-bust cycles of a capitalist economy, and the developing power of labor unions that were themselves aided considerably by state intervention.

Underlying the improved material state of the laborers, however, is the expansion of industrial production. To return to our illustration of the poodjet factory: Over the history of the factory, conflicts between workers and management largely concerned disagreement over wages. That is, the issue was the distribution of the proceeds from the sale of poodjets, and not worker input regarding the particulars of the poodjet production process. These conflicts have always been resolved by making and selling more poodjets; both sides have historically been satisfied with the *same share of greater proceeds*. This was not the result achieved by our well-meaning CEO. Since overall growth is the only option available to labor to secure increases in wages, labor must support growth, despite the greater environmental degradation that accompanies it.

Another reason why the working class remains a partner in the growth coalition is their lack of control over jobs. It is the corporate class that makes decisions affecting jobs—what kind and how many—not simply in their own industries, which are major employers in themselves, but indirectly for society as a whole. A decision to lay off several thousand workers at an auto plant, for example, will affect numerous other businesses and industries that supply the plant and its workforce. Corporate decisions to invest or disinvest have a ripple effect on employment that goes well beyond the particular company or its community. Similarly, the choice of corporations to move abroad—where wages are lower, regulations less restrictive, and profits therefore higher—have significant effects on the entire workforce. In short, corporations have immense direct and indirect power to create jobs and, if necessary for their interests, to destroy them.

Control over jobs gives employers the power to intimidate. Workers, as well as communities, are offered only two options: give corporations what they want or face higher unemployment. Corporations warn the public that policies restricting corporate freedom and profits will inevitably cost people their jobs. This is job blackmail, a tactic corporations use to manipulate public opinion on issues ranging from military spending to urban development.

In their book *Fear at Work* (1982), Kazis and Grossman assert that environmental job blackmail is a particularly insidious form of job blackmail. In the past two decades, new environmental laws have been enacted to protect people on the job and in their communities by limiting the ability of employers to pollute and use resources. Corporate executives have responded to newly imposed environmental obligations by claiming that the regulations kill the economy by eliminating existing jobs and interfering with the creation of new ones. Charging that people must choose between jobs and environmental quality, corporate executives play on the fears of unemployment to alienate workers from environmentalists. Highly publicized conflicts between workers and environmentalists, such as those surrounding the construction of the Alaska oil pipeline and the commercial use of nuclear energy for electric power, have reinforced the perception that the interests of workers and environmentalists are contradictory. Thus, the growth coalition includes labor as an entrenched part of the economic structure.

SUMMARY

When widespread public support for environmental protection emerged in the 1970s, the Congress responded with twenty-three major pieces of legislation. Structures were established for carrying out environmental policies that threatened corporate violators with penalties and other punishments that would reduce corporate profits. Such legislative actions averted a more serious legitimacy crisis for the state, but the laws were relatively weak and seldom enforced. In his study of laws governing corporations, Stone summarizes the effectiveness of regulatory processes: "The overall picture is that our strategies, aimed to control corporations by threatening their profits, are a very limited way of bringing about the internal changes that are necessary if the policies behind the law are to be effectuated" (1975:57).

Although the state, the corporations, and the working class all substantially contribute to and support economic growth, the growth coalition is not without fissures, and resistance to environmental degradation has periodically emerged. Today's environmental movement has its well-springs in the Progressive era of the early twentieth century. That early form of the environmental movement attempted to alter the corporate state's exploitation of the environment. It is to that history of economic growth and environmental resistance, and its implications for grassroots environmental conflict, that we now turn.

5. Keeping the Faith: Economic Growth and Environmental Exploitation

Throughout most of U.S. history, cultural beliefs regarding economic growth, as well as preferences for a higher standard of living, defused any sustained opposition that would seriously challenge the state's role in environmental matters. Nonetheless, environmental concerns have been episodically addressed in the past, most often by a politically involved middle class.

When corporations and the state were perceived as violating the public interest, criticism most consistently came from upper and middle-class activists who organized and acted as an interest group. *Interest groups* are generally defined by sociologists as voluntary organizations composed of people who share a similar attitude (interest), make special claims on other social groups, and serve as intermediaries between individuals and government. They also work within and are a normative component of the established political structure. Although interest groups may challenge a particular policy, they do not challenge the system itself. Typically, interest group members are either elites themselves or are so closely aligned with elites that their social ties afford them easy and routine access to the powerful.

In this chapter, we take a brief trek through U.S. history, examining the shared interests of business and the state in promoting economic growth at the expense of the environment. Beginning with the sixteenth-century European colonization of North America and progressing through the military-industrial complex of the latter half of the twentieth century, we look at the environmental consequences of many economic decisions and policies and we observe how, occasionally, the state's fulfillment of its accumulation function contradicted its legitimization function and aroused some form of environmental protest.

EUROPEAN COLONIZATION AND THE EARLY UNITED STATES

Native Americans occupied the North American continent for thousands of years before the European colonists arrived. They lived in harmony with nature, according to their spiritual beliefs that people were a part of nature and that land could not be owned. Viewing themselves as stewards of the earth, Native Americans lived within the boundaries of nature.

When the Europeans began colonization in North America in the sixteenth century, their discovery of the great abundance of natural resources fostered a "frontier" worldview in which resources were believed to be limitless. European colonists were imbued with the Judeo-Christian tradition, which provided a biblical justification for an *anthropocentric* view of the environment (White 1967). In an anthropocentric view, people are seen as the central focus—the most important species—of the natural world, and all other forms of life exist solely for the benefit of people. Judeo-Christian tenets, particularly Protestantism, encouraged the belief that nature is subservient to human needs, that people hold mastery over nature. The Europeans prized conquest and subjugation over coexistence and did not recognize the interdependence of human life and the physical environment. Protestantism, then, provided an intellectual foundation for environmental exploitation that was consonant with the principles of a capitalist economy. As a result, the capitalist economic system quickly reduced the environment of the North American continent to a huge warehouse of resources, which simply awaited a human hand to turn them to good use: the accumulation of wealth.

Yet concern for the management, if not the protection, of the environment did occasionally appear. In 1681 William Penn, given "ownership" of Pennsylvania by the British monarch, mandated that for every 5 acres of land cleared, 1 acre remain forested. In 1710 the Massachusetts Colony enacted ordinances to protect waterfowl in the coastal regions, and in this period the Connecticut and New York colonies regulated the hunting of various game animals. When the American Revolution ended and elections were established in 1789, the newly formed federal government assumed the role Great Britain had played in managing North American land resources. U.S. founders envisioned the role of government as the primary supporter of the economic development of the continent. Solutions to environmental problems under the frontier worldview simply meant finding new environments to exploit, rather than conserving the old environment.

Charles Darwin's work in the mid-1800s stimulated a change in public attitudes toward the environment. Building on the work of others, Darwin elaborated on the concepts of resource scarcity and ecosystem and emphasized the absolute dependence of all life on the physical environment. The previous, religious view of nature and the environment was gradually displaced in the nineteenth century by a more secular perspective.

Several efforts were made in the nineteenth century to preserve parts of the environment. In 1864 the Yosemite Valley of California was reserved as a state park; in 1872 Yellowstone National Park was established;

and in the 1870s the federal government created the U.S. Fish Commission, the U.S. Geological Survey, and the Department of Agriculture's Division of Forestry.

The attitudinal change stimulated by Darwin's work might have brought about a genuine environmental awareness, except for the explosive social change wrought by the Industrial Revolution. The Industrial Revolution struck the United States in the 1870s with the force of a social hurricane, as it had decades earlier in Great Britain. Radical changes in production processes reaped quantum leaps in economic growth. The benefits of economic growth effectively squelched any large-scale burgeoning of environmental concern that might have bloomed from the emergent secularized view of human-environment interdependence.

After the Civil War, rampant and unregulated capitalism led to massive violations of natural systems and to subsequently huge increases in environmental problems. Natural resources were extracted from the earth with no regard for environmental impacts, leading to some devastating environmental catastrophes. For example, exploitative logging practices near the end of the nineteenth century led to two terrible fires, one in 1871 in Wisconsin and another in 1894 in Minnesota. Logging also contributed to the infamous Johnstown, Pennsylvania, flood of 1889.

Thus, despite rare instances of pro-environment activities, the general thrust of the nation's activities was to sacrifice the environment for economic growth and private wealth. Although the laissez-faire model of business-government relations was never actually realized, reality most closely approached the model during the period of rapid industrial growth following the Civil War. Industrial expansion in this era was characterized by the unrelenting and generally successful efforts of business to obtain favorable government policies. Many such policies intentionally maximized the corporations' exploitation of government-controlled resources such as land, minerals, and timber. Corporate involvement in government often included the active role of corporate executives in politics, who strongly resisted attempts at government control and regulation. They found generally sympathetic ears: in the late 1880s, the U.S. Senate was called the "Millionaires' Club" because its membership included so many industrialists. This was so at a time when the average annual income in the United States was $573.

PROGRESSIVE CONSERVATIONISM

The unregulated environmental/economic binge of the Industrial Revolution eventually spawned the environmental movement known as progressive conservationism, a movement that grew as a reaction to the massive environmental destruction by industrialists. The destruction—reckless clearcutting, unreclaimed strip mining—combined with poor sanitation and heedless industrial air and water pollution in the fast-growing cities generated broad-based public support for efforts to curb the excessive abuses of the private ownership of resources. Characteristic of the progressives was the belief that the federal government should exercise its power, not only on behalf of private interests, but also in the public interest. Conservationists stressed the need for resource management and urged the institution of scientific management criteria in the use of natural resources.

Besides the wholesale environmental destruction committed by business with the government's blessing, other factors contributed to the growth of progressive conservationism, notably, the closing of the frontier and the recognition of the extensiveness of federal landholdings.

In 1890 the U.S. Census Bureau announced the formal closing of the American frontier, declaring that it no longer existed as a definable line. Because the frontier had always been an important symbol of the material abundance of North America, its closing shook people's beliefs in the limitlessness of nature. At the same time, the federal government owned 80 percent of the total land area of the United States, much of it simply confiscated from Native Americans. Thus, the closing of the frontier and the awareness of the federal government's significant land wealth combined with the economic exploitation of the environment to generate an organized and political environmental movement. Composed primarily of upper class citizens concerned about the rapid disposition of the public lands to corporations and the destruction of recreational lands for the sake of corporations, this early environmental movement urged the government to preserve some federal lands. In response, in 1891 the government established Yosemite National Park and enacted the Forest Reserve Act. The conservationists' environmental concern became part of the Progressive era of the late nineteenth and early twentieth centuries.

During the Progressive era, several organizations were created to promote progressive conservation. A number of them are still in existence today, including the Sierra Club (1892), the American Scenic and Historic Preservation Society (1895), the Society of American Foresters (1900), and the National Audubon Society (1905). The federal government responded to the concerns of these organizations with a number of legislative acts: the Forest Management Act (1897); the River and Harbor Act (1899), regulating pollution in navigable waterways for the first time; the Reclamation Act (1902), creating the Bureau of Reclamation; and the Antiquities Act (1906), defining a legal basis for preserving federal lands as national monuments.

The progressive conservation movement eventually split into two factions over environmentalists' differing views of economic growth and development. These disagreements among groups of environmental advocates demonstrate the important connection between the expansion of industrial production and the use or abuse of natural resources. Dominating one wing of the movement were the "preservationists," who emphasized *preservation*—the complete protection of undeveloped habitats from economic development. In contrast, members of the other wing were "conservationists"—supporters of the regulated use of public lands for economic growth through government-issued permits for mining, lumbering, grazing, and hydroelectric power generation. President Theodore Roosevelt's conservation policies represented a compromise between the preservationists and the conservationists, although, ultimately, the conservationist wing prevailed, as did their expansionist values. Thus, the pursuit of economic growth continued to supersede the protection of the environment.

A major consequence of the progressive conservation movement was the federal government's increased involvement in the economy. This early environmental movement has typically been depicted as a grassroots movement opposed to the power and privilege of large corporations, but that was not the case at all. In his book, *Conservation and the Gospel of Efficiency: The Progressive Conservation Movement, 1890–1920* (1959), Samuel P. Hays writes: "Conservation neither arose from a broad popular outcry, nor centered its fire primarily upon the private corporations. In fact, it becomes clear that one must discard completely the struggle against corporations as the setting in which to understand conservation history. Moreover, corporations often supported conservation policies, while the 'people' just as frequently opposed them."

It must be emphasized that, during the Progressive era, environmentalists typically came from affluent backgrounds. They were elites themselves, and they acted as an interest group rather than as a grassroots movement, pressuring state and federal legislators to preserve parts of public lands. Participation of almost any kind in the political process is much more characteristic of the higher than the lower classes. The interest group system, in particular, is overwhelmingly dominated by corporate and other upper class groups, with its members tending to be better educated, wealthier, and of higher social status. Interest groups may indeed compete with one another to have their desires met by the state, but the competition is among elite interest groups. Conservationists such as Theodore Roosevelt and Gifford Pinchot, appointed by Roosevelt as first chief of the U.S. Forest Service and later elected governor of Pennsylvania, were not ordinary working people campaigning to protect natural resources. Instead, they were politically powerful elites with easy access to the political process and, consequently, they were in an excellent position to influence that process.

Although the government's response to the progressive conservation movement—to hold some land in the public domain—appears to have been a public rather than a private benefit, it reduced the overall amount of resources available in the nation. In effect, then, government policy protected the economic status of already established corporations, holding a certain percentage of resources in trust for those with access, and made it difficult for new corporations to emerge. In a similar way, only the largest lumber companies, mining operations, and ranchers could afford the more recent technological innovations for extracting and processing resources. This economic efficiency appealed to the federal regulatory agencies that were charged with monitoring and maintaining the "wise use" of natural resources. As a result, regulatory agency policies tended to benefit larger operators more than smaller ones. Consequently, executives of the larger corporations were generally supportive of environmental progressivism as a conservative policy that protected and even enlarged their own wealth and power (Humphrey and Buttel 1982).

During this time, the government's principal function became the securing of a stable pattern of economic growth. Because of its commitment to economic growth, the government's environmental legislation frequently corresponded with the desires of corporations. A significant legacy of the early environmental movement was the symbiotic relationship that emerged between business and government. Thus, progressive conservationism was led by and represented the interests of elites. The elite movement had two important consequences: (1) it contributed to the concentration of wealth in the hands of large corporations; and (2) it set in motion the trend of government-augmented economic growth, with the unintended, and ironic, consequences of environmental degradation. Progressive conservation significantly shaped public and private attitudes about economic growth, pollution, and resource scarcities in the first seven decades of this century.

THE GREAT DEPRESSION

The 1930s brought about a change in the relationship between government and corporations that further reinforced their symbiotic roles. The most serious economic depression in U.S. history, the Great Depression generated the government's active role as a *creator* of economic policy rather than as a mere shaper of it. Government intervention in the economy during the Great Depression became even more direct. Influenced by the economic theories of John Maynard Keynes, the federal government under the administration of Franklin D. Roosevelt activated a sweeping series of measures to stabilize the boom-then-bust business cycle that characterizes capitalist economies. Implemented during an emergency, Roosevelt's actions cemented the relationship between government and corporations and accelerated the sacrifice of environmental resources to the engine of expanding economic growth.

Earlier economic depressions in the United States, the results of relatively smaller fluctuations in the business cycle, had reversed themselves naturally. In contrast, the Great Depression did not reverse itself at all, and the economy continued to stagnate. The predominant Keynesian economic analysts argued that, since jobs depended on production and production could not increase without consumer demand for the products, the government must intervene to stimulate consumption through spending programs and tax cuts. (Conversely, the theory stated, in a time when consumer demand was excessive and inflation threatened economic stability, the government must reverse its policies by cutting expenditures and raising taxes.) In adopting these policies, the government assumed substantial and unprecedented responsibility for monitoring and stabilizing the economic system. Government became a full partner in business to further the economic growth that would maintain the legitimacy of the state.

In all of this turmoil the environment was not forgotten, for the Great Depression also had the effect of drawing the attention of many citizens to the need to maintain the physical, environmental basis of economic growth. Conservation was a more important public issue than it had been since the first decade of the century, and in the late 1930s the Wilderness Society and the National Wildlife Federation were founded.

The government's expanded role in land and resource management during the Great Depression clearly highlights the connection between economic growth and the use of the environment. Within two months in 1933, Congress passed two bills sponsored by Roosevelt that are among the best known laws in American conservation history: the Civilian Conservation Corps (CCC) and the Tennessee Valley Authority (TVA). A brief description of each shows the linkages between economic growth and the environment, and the federal government's acute awareness of those linkages.

The CCC was designed to revive local economies and to provide productive work for nearly two million unemployed young men. The CCC also reflected a national desire to repair some of the environmental damage inflicted in three centuries of economic exploitation. In his call to Congress to pass the bill, Roosevelt said: "[T]his type of work is of definite, practical value, not only through the prevention of great present financial loss, but also as a means of creating future national wealth. [The CCC will] conserve our precious natural resources. It will make improvements in national and state domains which have been largely forgotten in the past few years of industrial development" (Nash 1990: 140–141).

Between 1933 and 1942, when it was abolished by Congress, the CCC participated in a wide variety of environmental projects. The young men planted nearly one billion trees, constructed countless roads and fire detection facilities, controlled soil erosion, developed new park and recreation areas, restored silted waterways, provided flood control, controlled insects and protected wildlife. Their work consistently dealt with projects of public, rather than private, interest. Yet successful businessmen, worried that government action would change the market factors that had made them successful, insisted that, by government mandate, CCC activities be *noncompetitive with private industry*.

The second New Deal law, and a landmark in U.S. conservation history, created the TVA. A history of the founding of the TVA is also the history of a thirty-year national debate over the appropriateness of public versus private electric power generation. This debate, again, illustrates the connection between economic development and environmental use. Today's electric power industry grew from two mutually hostile traditions: a *private* tradition, in which entrepreneurs risked capital and reaped huge financial benefits, and a *public* tradition, in which advocates of public-controlled power tried to regulate financial excesses in the private power industry, sometimes by going into the power business themselves.

The control of electric power generation was a critical issue because of the enormous amounts of power needed to run production processes. By the early part of the twentieth century, power transmission technology had made it possible to transport electric power from remote rivers to urban industrial centers. A number of conservationists feared that, if private utility corporations were permitted to monopolize all hydroelectric sites, the utility industry would take control of all industry and eventually the nation. Consequently, many conservationists advocated a public-controlled power industry.

The issue of electric power technology led to a struggle among conservationists, preservationists, and private utility corporations. The utility corporations and the preservationists found themselves in an uneasy alliance, supporting private power generation against the conservationists' support of public power. As was the case with the eventual curtailing of the CCC's projects, the primary issue in the power controversy was whether the federal government should compete with private industry. The utility corporations were opposed to government competition because it would decrease or eliminate their profits. The preservationists, the temporary allies of the utility corporations, were opposed to government competition in electric power generation because it would mean sacrificing preserved public lands for the dams and reservoirs needed to construct hydroelectric plants.

An important focal point for the controversy over public versus private power was the development of the federally owned Muscle Shoals site on the Tennessee River. At Muscle Shoals, Alabama, the Tennessee River falls 137 feet in 37 miles, making it the most important water-power site of the entire, enormous Tennessee River system. Private developers wanted to purchase the site from the government to build a hydroelectric plant, but the National Defense Act of 1916 stipulated that the facilities at Muscle Shoals were to be used by the government to produce nitrates. Nitrates were needed during wartime for explosives and during peacetime for fertilizers.

The nitrate plants built at Muscle Shoals were not made operational during World War I. When President Woodrow Wilson attempted to carry out the mandate of the act after the First World War, his plan became enmeshed in the dispute over public versus private operation of hydroelectric plants. Several companies tried to buy the Muscle Shoals region for private development, but their efforts were consistently foiled by prominent Nebraska conservationist and U.S. Senator George W. Norris.

Norris sponsored a federal bill for the multipurpose development of the Tennessee River by the government for the purposes of national defense, navigation, electric power generation, flood control, and fertilizer production. Although Congress passed the bill in 1928, President Coolidge pocket-vetoed it. Congress passed the bill again in 1930, but President Hoover vetoed it amid charges that the bill was socialist. The legislation was finally passed in 1933 as a part of Roosevelt's New Deal legislation to bolster economic development. Thus, the TVA was created as the first public regional development agency charged with assisting regional economic development while protecting natural resources. As such, the TVA was a microcosm of the federal government, charged with the conflicting obligations of facilitating economic growth while maintaining the environment.

WORLD WAR II

World War II brought changes that significantly influenced the government's support of economic growth and the public's acceptance of that support. Wartime production finally carried the nation out of the Great Depression. The war mobilized and concentrated capitalist efforts in military production: the massive building of bombs, tanks, jeeps, airplanes, and all the other material goods needed to sustain the war effort.

The relationship between government and industry which supplied the needs of war became the foundation of postindustrial capitalism. Although the government funds military production, the production processes are carried out by private corporations that consequently reap tremendous financial benefits with very little risk. Thus, the military production required for World War II made many corporate owners rich. The economic success realized in military production strengthened cultural beliefs in social progress through economic growth. The militarized economy that emerged during World War II was further developed through the Korean conflict, the cold war, and the Vietnam War. Citing the threat posed by the Soviet Union and the Eastern Bloc countries and warning of impending layoffs of thousands of workers, the Reagan administration further heightened military production. War has provided an important addition to the mutual dependence of state and corporation, and military production has produced a stable floor of jobs and profits for the rest of the economy that postwar leaders have found prudent to sustain.

Wartime advancements in technology for radar and the airplane convinced many people that technological investment was the most efficient means for continuing economic growth. Postwar families therefore counted on technological advances to make the American Dream come true.

Yet many of the technological advances made during World War II have had deleterious effects on the environment because they led to production methods that shifted the emphasis away from labor-intensive toward more energy-intensive technologies that use synthetic chemicals as substitutes for natural resources. Energy-intensive production technologies disturb ecosystems in two important ways. First, they require much higher levels of energy, depleting nonrenewable energy sources at a much faster rate and so threatening economic growth. Second, in their use of synthetic organic chemicals, production processes generate greater levels of chemical and other potentially harmful wastes. These potentially dangerous wastes enter the environment and the food chain with often toxic consequences.

The bottom line is that corporations profited enormously using the new energy-intensive production methods, and economic growth reached unprecedented levels. Thus, rather than curbing the technological trend in order to protect the environment, the government actively supported the new technologies through public investment in technological policies, taxation for science and technology education, grants for technological research, and direct agency research.

The convergence between the federal government and the corporate class grew after World War II, with the result that the corporate state became stronger than ever. Corporations favored the rise of big government and its intervention in economic affairs, regarding government, not as a threat to their activities but as an ally, as a guarantor of a stable economy and an important consumer of corporate products and services. In a similar way, government officials accepted the inevitability and the advantageousness of supporting the large corporate enterprise as the dominant form of business. A healthy political atmosphere for the election of officials required a healthy economic atmosphere which, in turn, came to depend on the corporation's sustained well-being.

POSTWAR AMERICA AND THE MILITARY-INDUSTRIAL COMPLEX

Corporate class interests continued to prosper in the postwar years as a result of their close alliance with the federal government. Little opposition emerged to environmental exploitation in the name of economic growth. In addition to an increased faith in economic growth and the closer merger of the state and the corporate class, World War II left another legacy: the cold war and the subsequent economic boost of constant military production.

Over three decades ago, former general and President Dwight D. Eisenhower warned the public against the creation of an all-powerful military-industrial complex. He cautioned that in defense spending the critical issue is how much the country can spend without jeopardizing other social benefits. Eisenhower's concern involved revenues that were being taken away from social programs to fuel the weapons industry. With finite funds, trade-offs were inevitable: a warship instead of food for the poor, a rocket instead of college scholarships. Directing the efforts of scientists and laborers toward war directed their efforts away from peace.

Yet military production was, and is, both secure from risk and lucrative, and a stable source of employment. Society at large, however, pays for this symbiotic relationship between industry and the military through the environmental consequences of producing and deploying modern weapons, from the mining of the raw materials to the eventual disposal of the wastes.

The U.S. military is likely the largest generator of hazardous wastes in the country and probably the world (Renner 1991; Van Voorst 1992). Military installations cover 25.6 million acres in the United States. For decades the armed forces have allowed leaking of oil and other fuels, draining of toxic chemicals into waterways, dumping of lethal sludge at unlined landfills, and littering of the countryside with unexploded shells and bombs. In many cases where military bases sit astride local water sources, some neighboring towns have detected higher incidences of tumors, cancer, and birth defects (Van Voorst 1992). In recent years, the Pentagon has generated more toxics than the top five U.S. chemical corporations combined—about 400,000 to 500,000 tons of toxics annually (Renner 1991). Within the United States, the number of sites on which problems have been spotted increased from 3526 sites on 529 military bases in 1986 to 14,401 sites on 1579 bases in 1989. Almost 100 bases are already on the Superfund list, and the EPA estimates that as many as 1000 military sites will be added to the list (Renner 1991).

Nuclear weapons production and testing have had a more severe and enduring impact on the environment than any other military operation, and nuclear weapons have been the area of the strongest government-industrial collaboration. The first U.S. nuclear weapons were developed by the U.S. Army's Manhattan Engineering District, or "Manhattan Project," during World War II. Following the war, all control of atomic energy was turned over to the Atomic Energy Commission, established by the Atomic Energy Act of 1946. The act limits private ownership of fissionable material and classifies as restricted data all information relating to the development of nuclear weapons. It also provides for civilian rather than military control over the development of nuclear warheads and naval reactors.

After the war and during the 1950s, the federal government waged an "Atoms for Peace" campaign to promote the peaceful uses of atomic energy. Under this campaign, the government initiated the commercial nuclear power industry. In order to bolster a reluctant commercial nuclear power industry, the Atomic Energy Act was amended in 1954 to allow the private ownership of nuclear materials, and in 1957 the Price-Anderson Act limited corporate liabilities for nuclear accidents. Many civilian-owned reactors were in operation by the 1960s. In 1974 Congress split the Atomic Energy Commission into the Nuclear Regulatory Commission (NRC), which was established to regulate commercial applications of nuclear energy, and the Energy Research and Development Administration (ERDA), which was given charge of nuclear weapons activities and research relating to energy technology. In 1977, under President Carter, ERDA became the Department of Energy. Military expenditures increased further during the Reagan and Bush administrations.

Nuclear warheads are designed and built by the U.S. Department of Energy (DOE), dozens of corporations, and several universities at seventeen major sites in thirteen states. Although the weapons facilities are owned by the federal government, the plants are operated by more than seventy contractors that bid for DOE work. Among the contractors at the government-owned contractor-operated facilities are some of the largest U.S. corporations, such as General Electric, Monsanto, and Westinghouse, as well as major universities, including the University of California and the University of Chicago.

Because of a combination of poor recordkeeping, loss, damage, and the ever present multipurpose cloak of national security, a definitive catalog of environmental problems stemming from military nuclear production processes does not exist. Some dangers are known, however. Beginning in the 1950s, many rights were sacrificed to expedience in the desperation of the cold war, and the brisk buildup of nuclear arsenals was given unambiguous precedence over the health and safety of workers, soldiers, and residents. For decades, officials knowingly subjected their own unsuspecting citizens to the dangers of radioactivity in the name of national security. Military nuclear reactors are responsible for an estimated 97 percent of all high-level nuclear waste and 78 percent of all low-level nuclear waste, by volume. It has been estimated that more than fifty bombs, equal to the one dropped on Nagasaki, could be manu-factured just from the waste that has leaked from the underground waste tanks storage at the government's nuclear facility in Hanford, Washington.

DOE's nuclear weapons production facilities occupy twice as much land as the state of Delaware and employ more than 90,000 people. Since the 1940s, the weapons complex has produced some 60,000 warheads, over one-third of which are currently in the arsenal. During more than forty years of weapons production, the United States has spent about $104.5 billion ($250 billion in 1988 dollars) on the manufacture of nuclear warheads and another $800 billion ($1.95 trillion in 1988 dollars) on delivery systems and other support costs.

Other, nonnuclear toxic wastes from weapons production include fu-els, paints, solvents, heavy metals, pesticides, PCBs, cyanides, phenols, acids, alkalies, propellants, and explosives. These wastes are suspected of causing cancer, birth defects, and chromosomal damage and of seriously impairing the function of people's liver, kidneys, blood, and central ner-vous system.

The cost of repairing the damage already done by permanent war preparation will be staggering. Nuclear decontamination costs are esti-mated to be $2 million for every nuclear warhead the nation has pro-duced. Many of the aged production facilities operated by DOE are in disrepair, and a number are shut down because of safety problems. Virtu-ally all the plants are plagued with massive chemical and radioactive waste contamination.

Even if no more warheads are produced, Americans now face the enormous task of cleaning up the production sites and safely disposing of radioactive and toxic chemical wastes. The problems and costs of environ-mental cleanup at federal nuclear facilities have been aggravated by years of neglect. In 1978 President Jimmy Carter issued an executive order that instructed the military to comply with environmental legislation, but the order was not enforced. In 1980 Congress passed the Comprehensive Environmental Response, Compensation and Liability Act (CERCLA or Superfund law), which made corporate polluters responsible for cleaning up hazardous wastes, but the departments of Defense and Energy de-clared themselves exempt under the directives assigned to them by the Atomic Energy Act. They were left largely self-regulated.

The year 1988 marked a watershed for problems in the nuclear weap-ons production complex. Headlines in newspapers and lead stories on the nightly news focused public attention on the massive safety and environmental problems that have festered for decades at the seventeen sites that make up the complex. A string of reports by DOE and the General Accounting Office made it clear that the cost of fixing the problems could exceed $150 billion. Actual expenditures, however, were far more forthcoming to bail out the savings and loan industry, the year's other crisis.

Also in 1988, DOE released its plan for rebuilding and cleaning up the weapons complex. In the void left by the disintegration of the Soviet Union, DOE in its Modernization Report proposed to spend almost $50 billion between 1990 and 2010 to convert today's weapons complex into a complex for the next century, including the construction, relocation, and/ or renovation of a number of weapons production plants. The plan, however, devotes far less money—less than half of total estimated needs—to the cleanup of serious contamination across the complex. As a result, significant threats to the environment will remain unaddressed in 2010, when the modernized weapons complex is expected to be completed.

Besides the huge financial costs are the social costs—the contamination of communities and the exposure of citizens to harmful substances. Increasingly, local communities, appalled at revelations about military pollution, are clamoring for information about what is going on in their neighborhoods and are demanding that the Pentagon be made accountable. In September 1992 Congress passed the Federal Facilities Act that places federal facilities under the same environmental enforcement regimen as the civilian sector, making federal violators liable for the same fines. It has been proposed that the technological resources of the Defense Department be marshaled to address environmental problems, but no technology can be applied to the problem until the political and social decision to apply it has been made.

SUMMARY

From the sixteenth-century European colonization of North America through the 1950s, the American public has generally retained its faith in the doctrine of economic growth, frequently at the expense of the environment. As a result, the corporate state has grown steadily more robust, with the links between the two social institutions so intertwined that neither would likely survive without the other.

Occasionally, this formidable force for economic growth provoked some opposition, but the opposition was mostly reform-oriented, representing an interest group that presented no challenge to the essential social structure. And, most importantly, the opposition consisted of insiders—people within and part of the power structure itself. The grievances of these upper and upper middle-class elites, active in the Progressive era and again during the Great Depression, involved wilderness and preservation issues. Production processes and the state's support of private profit were not seriously questioned.

The cold war provided the corporate state alliance with both a rationale for continued environmental neglect and a reliable, prodigal, and uncritical market that has provided a measure of stability to a previously erratic economy. And so the public kept the faith—for a while longer.

6. *Rumblings from Below*

Although the federal government continued its emphasis on economic growth at the expense of the environment into the 1960s, for the first time since the Great Depression the state's actions were influenced by environmentalists. Rather than conservationist efforts of the 1930s, environmentalism in this era took the form of national-based environmental organizations engaged in lobbying for environmental legislation. These national organizations, many of which had been in existence for some time, formed what is popularly understood as the contemporary environmental movement.

While charges of elitism in the movement raised the issue of social class, the debate raged only within the confines of the movement itself, not significantly touching the lives of nonactivists. The national environmental organizations continued to lobby and to wear the mantle of the environmental movement, claiming to represent all those concerned with environmental quality. Faith in the doctrine of economic growth remained strong. Then in the late 1970s, events occurred that prompted a wave of doubt. The efforts of the national environmental organizations were of little help, and it appeared that the environmental movement might actually be two class-based movements.

In this chapter we continue our history of the relationships among economic growth, environmental exploitation, and the corporate state by examining the contemporary environmental movement. After discussing the movement's emergence, composition, and goals, we focus in detail on two events that have had a profound impact, not only on the environmental movement, but also on our cultural and political systems.

NATIONAL ENVIRONMENTAL LOBBYING ORGANIZATIONS

The contemporary environmental movement, dominant from about 1964 to 1978, emerged in part as a response to the postwar shift in production technologies to more energy-intensive methods. The nega-

67

tive impacts of the new production technologies increased environmental concerns among many people and broadened the conception of resource conservation to include the preservation of the quality of the air, water, and soil.

An important catalyst of the contemporary environmental movement was the 1962 publication of Rachel Carson's *Silent Spring*. Carson, a marine biologist with the U.S. Fish and Wildlife Service and a nature writer, described the concerns of some scientists about the widespread use of DDT and other long-lasting pesticides used in agricultural programs. Her book not only influenced other scientists and professionals, but also had significant political impact. The chemical industry attempted to discredit the book and malign Carson, but their efforts misfired when the negative publicity that the industry deliberately generated about her book actually drew people's attention to it all the more. Impressed by his reading of *Silent Spring*, President John F. Kennedy appointed a special panel of his Science Advisory Committee to study the problem of pesticides. The committee's subsequent report substantiated Carson's argument. The book became a best-seller and helped to make the previously unfamiliar word *ecology* a significant popular cause.

The federal government responded to these stirrings of environmental concern by enacting a series of laws: the Clean Air Act (1963); the Wilderness Act (1964), which established the National Wilderness Preservation System; the National Historic Preservation Act (1966); and the Endangered Species Act (1966), which initiated federal involvement in habitat protection and rare species identification.

After 1960, the term *environmentalism* replaced *conservationism*. The late 1960s counterculture, the "hippie generation," which already questioned the traditional ideals and priorities of mainstream middle-class U.S. culture, probably contributed to environmentalism's popularity. This youth movement stressed community and simplicity over individualism and economic gain. Such values are consistent with protection of the environment.

Environmental sociologists Craig Humphrey and Fred Buttel note the speed with which environmentalism rose to prominence among the public. They cite Gallup polls showing that, between 1965 and 1970, concern about air and water pollution grew from about 15 percent to about 53 percent (1982). Several events occurred during this period that bolstered environmental concerns. Then, in 1968 Paul Ehrlich published *The Population Bomb*, in which he suggested that world population growth is the cause of not only environmental pollution but also a number of other social problems. At this time, serious concerns were voiced about the links between human health and welfare and the protection of nature. Some feared that a careless technological civilization could impact catastrophically on the health of the entire biosphere.

Such fears were intensified by the astronauts' first photographs of "Spaceship Earth." In 1968 U.S. astronauts first orbited the moon and brought back dramatic photographs and breathless descriptions of the tiny, blue sphere in the immensity of space, carrying all known life in its precious skin. The fragility of that spaceship was made all the more apparent by the 1969 oil spill off the coast of Santa Barbara, California. Two mishaps at an offshore oil rig, and the Santa Barbara beach was suddenly transformed into an alien landscape in which oil-coated fish were washed up on shore and birds and otters struggled in the oily muck and died. Television carried these images into homes, igniting greater environmental concern among the public.

Concurrent with the upswing in environmental concern was the emergence of new environmental organizations. In 1967 the Environmental Defense Fund was organized; in 1969 Greenpeace emerged; and in 1970 the Natural Resources Defense Council and Zero Population Growth were founded. The culmination of this environmental concern was manifested at the popular level in the first Earth Day, celebrated on April 22, 1970, and at the legal level in the congressional action that transformed the 1970s into the "Environmental Decade." Beginning with the trail-blazing National Environmental Policy Act of 1970, Congress passed more than two dozen pieces of legislation to protect air, water, land, and wildlife. In fact, Congress continued to grind out environmental laws even after popular enthusiasm for environmental causes had waned considerably. Although the flurry of environmental legislation lasted until the 1978 National Energy Act, active popular support of environmental issues declined significantly with the mid-1970s energy crisis and economic recession. That is, environmental concern decreased when economic issues came into competition with them.

The energy crisis struck directly at economic growth because petroleum is the basis for production processes. In October 1973 the Organization of Petroleum Exporting Countries (OPEC), taking a page from the industrialized nation's book, announced that it was initiating an oil embargo and demanded higher oil prices. Oil prices had remained at the same unnaturally low level for over twenty years. OPEC's plan was to reduce supplies in order to increase price. The resultant oil shortage was followed by higher oil prices and led to gas rationing and occasionally some episodes of violence at the gas pumps. Only a few environmentalists saw the violence as a portent or acknowledged the long-term significance of the oil crisis: that, even if the present crisis was a contrivance, it was obvious that eventually the oil really would be gone. In a national survey at the time of the crisis, most U.S. adult citizens agreed that environmental regulations should be relaxed if energy shortages and energy price increases persisted (Bartell 1976).

Congressional action on environmental matters continued, but several indicators suggest that congressional members were also feeling the pinch between the rock of the economy and the hard place of environmental protection. Intermingled with such laws as the Endangered Species Act (1973), the Toxic Substances Control Act (1976), and the Surface Mining Control and Reclamation Act (1977) were pieces of legislation that revealed the government's concerns about the economy. In 1973, for example, Congress authorized an 800-mile oil pipeline that would cross Alaska to Prudhoe Bay, despite persistent and vociferous opposition by environmentalists. The Federal Land Policy and Management Act (1976) formalized multiple-use administration of public lands under the control of the Bureau of Land Management. ("Multiple use" is a euphemism for economic development.)

What resistance was offered to this emphasis on environmental exploitation and by whom? Considerable resistance through lobbying was brought by the national environmental organizations.

Description

The national-based organizations of the contemporary environmental movement are the natural successors to the progressive conservationist movement of the early twentieth century. In fact, three organizations remain unchanged today: the Sierra Club, the National Audubon Society, and the National Parks and Conservation Association. Perhaps the most significant similarity between the national-based segment of the contemporary environmental movement and the progressive conservation movement of the early twentieth century is that participants in both movements tended to be of high social class status. Historically, the environmental movement has been supported by the higher social class segment of the American population, especially among the white, male, educated, white-collar stratum. The primary constituency of today's national organizations continues to be white and middle class. Leaders and staff are almost exclusively white and most often male. Few of these organizations appealed to or recruited the working class, Native Americans, African-Americans, or Latinos.

The national environmental organizations have traditionally emphasized the protection of land and wildlife, stressing conservation. In the 1960s and 1970s some groups added toxics to their agendas but retained their primary commitment to conservation issues. Groups founded in this period devote some resources to air pollution, water pollution, and other toxic chemical problems, but frequently give less attention to the effects of toxics on human health than to general environmental quality.

Today twelve national environmental organizations dominate the contemporary environmental movement and focus most of their efforts on lobbying in Congress to change environmental policies and their implementation. The "Dominant Dozen" national environmental organizations are the Sierra Club, National Audubon Society, National Parks and Conservation Association, Izaak Walton League, Wilderness Society, National Wildlife Federation, Defenders of Wildlife, Environmental Defense Fund, Friends of the Earth, Natural Resources Defense Council, Environmental Action, and Environmental Policy Institute. Ten of those twelve organizations form the "Group of 10," or the "Big 10," consisting of group representatives who meet periodically in an informal coalition to discuss common strategies and problems. These organizations devote a large amount of time and resources to lobbying for environmental policies.

The national environmental groups focus most of their work on national legislation or litigation and view concrete changes in law or policy as the most important outcomes of their work. Although many organizations have local and state chapters, the resources of the organization are concentrated in their headquarters in Washington, D.C. The staffs typically contain a large proportion of scientists and lawyers who spend a considerable amount of time in court, Congress, or scientific meetings. These experts regularly interact with industry and government experts, with whom they share a professional training and an understanding of the rules of the political game. The experts have an important psychological, as well as practical, stake in preserving their credibility with other experts and with government decision makers. This stake may sometimes encourage them to compromise on particular issues in order to preserve both esteem and relationships that could be helpful in the future.

Tactically, the national environmental organizations prefer to instigate policy reform for the protection of the environment. To reform policy, the organizations engage in electoral campaigns, congressional and administrative lobbying, overseeing administrative decision making, and, when necessary, litigation. In all cases, the national organizations work completely within the system. Because they attempt to influence policy through traditional channels, they concentrate their efforts in Washington, D.C., where Congress and federal agencies rule on environmental policies.

A smaller number of national environmental organizations do not openly lobby. These are either direct groups such as Greenpeace USA and Earth First!, whose members engage in protest activities that are outside the system and even sometimes violate the law, or preservation associations such as the Nature Conservancy and World Wildlife Fund. Despite differences in tactics, these national nonlobbying organizations are similar to the lobbying organizations in social class and gender composition; members of both types of national groups tend to be white males of mid- to high social class status.

Environmental lobbyists play a crucial role in pressuring Congress and the various government agencies involved with environmental issues to enact new laws. Lobbying is viewed in the culture as a normal and an acceptable method of ensuring organized interest groups a meaningful role in lawmaking.

The national groups also try to influence the enforcement of existing laws. Laws typically leave a great deal of discretion to agencies in both setting standards and enforcing them. Agencies and affected parties subsequently engage in administrative proceedings to determine the appropriate implementation of the laws. Prior to the 1960s, environmentalists and citizens groups were not granted legal standing to participate in the administrative proceedings because the government agencies themselves were regarded as representing the public interest. Many analysts, however, claim that administrative law has moved closer to a system of interest representation in which all interested parties are recognized as having legal standing.

The environmental lobby, then, has the opportunity to press for strong standards and strict enforcement. Specifically, it assesses environmental impact statements, comments on proposed regulations, petitions for regulatory action when agencies have been too lax, participates in scientific advisory committees, provides information to the agencies, and testifies at administrative hearings. Such strategies are compatible with the environmental organizations' form of mobilization in which dues-paying members from all over the country delegate authority to the organizations in Washington, D.C., and provide them with the resources necessary for active lobbying. Additional funds for particular campaigns are solicited from members via sophisticated computer mailing systems.

Until the early 1960s, the national environmental organizations were fairly small and only occasionally lobbied in Congress; volunteers carried much of the administrative workload inasmuch as the number of paid staff was quite small. By the early 1970s, however, professionalism characterized the environmental organizations, particularly in the number of lobbyists, lawyers, and scientists employed full time. *Professionalism* refers to a style of organization characterized by the same features identified in many other formal organizations: a paid, professional staff and clearly defined roles for members who fill particular positions in the organization. Professionalism was also apparent in the organizations' planning exercises, budgets, and financial control. The organizations formalized their financial operations and hired professional fund-raisers. As a result of this professionalization process, however, the national organizations have been criticized for being less responsive to members, too eager to compromise, and more concerned about their annual budgets than about the environment.

Charges of Environmental Elitism

Most people think of the large national environmental organizations such as the Sierra Club when they hear about "the environmental movement." And for good reason: these organizations are quite visible. They "have several million dues-paying adherents; command multimillion-dollar budgets; employ corps of full-time lobbyists, lawyers, and scientists; and enjoy widespread support" (Mitchell, Mertig, and Dunlap 1992, p. 12). Many people, however, including some who have environmental sympathies, have accused the environmental movement, as it is represented by the Dominant Dozen, of being elitist. The issue of environmental elitism has been debated among environmentalists and academics from the earliest days of the contemporary environmental movement, the late 1960s.

Elitism is a serious charge and a very complex one. Morrison and Dunlap analyze the charge by identifying three categories of environmental elitism: compositional elitism, ideological elitism, and impact elitism (1986). *Compositional elitism* is the charge that the environmental movement is composed primarily of elites, of people from higher socioeconomic levels. *Ideological elitism* accuses environmentalists of pressing for environmental reforms that will benefit their own social group at the cost of those from lower socioeconomic levels. *Impact elitism* is the charge that reforms have more negative consequences for lower socioeconomic levels, whether or not environmentalists sought that effect.

Examining data on voluntary environmental organizations to assess charges of compositional elitism, Morrison and Dunlap find that "the modal member of an environmental organization is a college graduate, holds a professional-level job, and has an above-average income" (1986: 582). They conclude that members of environmental organizations are of the upper middle class; this is, in fact, characteristic of all types of political activists. Morrison and Dunlap emphasize the distinction between *members* of environmental organizations—activists—and *supporters* of environmental organizations—those who sympathize with environmentalism but are not themselves activists. Support for environmentalism among the public is not so strongly related to socioeconomic status as it is among organizational members.

Ideological elitism and impact elitism are most often derived from compositional elitism. That is, if the movement is overwhelmingly composed of activists from a particular social group, their ideology—their view of the world—likely reflects the interests of that social group. Adhering to an ideology that reflects one worldview probably results in actions that counter the interests of those with a different ideology. Although intentionality is a significant issue in charges of elitism, it has little relevance for the social group that bears the negative consequences of actions, since they must suffer the effects whether or not intended.

Thurow offers an explanation for environmental elitism, arguing that environmentalism is closely linked with income distribution because, as income rises and people are able to turn their attention to more than just physical survival, they begin to demand more goods and services. Environmentalism is, essentially, a demand for a particular good/service: a clean environment; thus, environmentalism derives from an increasing standard of living. For the privileged, a clean environment becomes "the next item on their acquisitive agenda" (Thurow 1980:105).

We conclude that the national environmental organizations are elitist to the extent that the leadership is composed primarily of white, middle-class males. Given the socioeconomic composition of the organizations, the interests of other socioeconomic groups such as the working class and poor may not be adequately represented by the national environmental organizations. This perception has become increasingly common since 1978.

Throughout U.S. history, citizens of all socioeconomic strata have been in general agreement with the government in the desire for continued economic growth. The lower social classes have traditionally been highly supportive of increasing economic growth, providing a critical segment of what Schnaiberg referred to as the growth coalition. When environmental conflicts occurred, they most often pitted a single, discrete act of pollution against jobs-in-general; that is, they required weighing one instance of pollution against the society's standard of living. Not surprisingly, most people chose the latter. As a consequence, the history of the twentieth-century environmental movement is overwhelmingly a portrait of formal organizations composed of white, educated, middle-, and upper class males engaged in lobbying the federal government to preserve pristine portions of the environment for recreational or scientific purposes, with some concern since the 1960s directed toward the improvement of environmental quality. Actual challenges to the corporate state power structure that perpetuates constantly increasing economic growth at the expense of the environment have been exceedingly few and spectacularly unsuccessful.

Then, at a relatively quiet moment in history, both faith in the doctrine of economic growth and abiding acceptance of the power structure were cracked. This phenomenon, rare as any creature on an endangered species list, occurred among some of the establishment's staunchest supporters: the working class. What event brought about such distrust of the system? Why did citizens become fearful that there was no safe place for their children? What happened to change the course of the contemporary environmental movement and offer an international stage for the playing out of deep-rooted class conflicts? Love Canal happened.

PORTENTS OF THE NEW PLAGUE

In a provocative opening to an anthology on environmental risks, sociologist Kai Erikson identifies a "new species of trouble" typified by recent events such as Love Canal, Three Mile Island, Bhopal, and Chernobyl. This new species of trouble is substantially different from the disasters faced by the ancients—drought, famine, flood, and plague: namely, it is created by humans, but they have little control over it. These new threats "involve toxic poisons, by which I mean that they contaminate rather than merely damage; that they pollute, befoul, taint, rather than just create wreckage; that they penetrate human tissue indirectly rather than wound the surfaces by assaults of a more straightforward kind. At their worst, these disasters can have a malevolence that the authors of Revelations would have found difficult to believe. And the evidence is growing that they scare human beings in new and special ways, that they elicit an uncanny fear in us" (Erikson 1991:15). The uncanny fear generated by the new species of trouble inspires a deep and profound dread: "pure dread, perfect dread, the very essence of dread" (Erikson 1991:12). Out of this dread, like Phoenix rising from the ashes, come resolution, action, and an altered political consciousness that gives the contemporary environmental movement a new and challenging orientation.

In August 1978 New York State health officials announced the "grave and imminent peril" posed to the residents of a working-class suburban community by the chemical landfill later known to the world as Love Canal. With this public pronouncement, the nature of the environmental movement changed significantly and emerged in a form that today is a familiar feature of the social landscape: grassroots environmental conflict.

Love Canal

Prior to the notoriety, the Love Canal neighborhood was just one working-class corner of the LaSalle section of the city of Niagara Falls, New York. Love Canal was named after William Love, a late nineteenth-century entrepreneur, who excavated a canal with the intention of providing free hydroelectric power to encourage the growth of his planned industrial community of Model City. The city never materialized, and in the 1930s Hooker Electrochemical Company (later Hooker Chemicals Corporation) bought the abandoned canal. Both Hooker Chemicals and the city used the canal as a dump site, depositing municipal and chemical wastes. After a decade of intensive dumping of well over 21,000 tons of chemical wastes in the canal, Hooker Chemicals in 1952 closed the landfill and covered it with a cap of indigenous soil.

In the following year, Hooker Chemicals sold the waste disposal site to the city of Niagara Falls for the token cost of $1. A subtle warning was issued in a disclaimer Hooker Chemicals included in the deed of sale, stipulating that the company was not responsible for any injury, death, or loss of property caused by the industrial wastes in the Love Canal. Despite the warning, the city built an elementary school on the 16-acre site. The presence of the school drew developers and contributed to the construction of a working-class neighborhood of owner-occupied, single-family homes. Houses were arrayed on neat grids of streets that radiated from the canal site.

In the 1950s individual residents occasionally complained to the city about strong odors, rocks that exploded when dropped, and skin irritations on the feet of children who played barefoot near the school. Their complaints were either ignored completely or treated with short-term remedial measures and dismissed.

In the 1960s residents' concerns increased. Homeowners complained to City Hall of a black oily substance oozing through the walls of their basements, which many attributed to the waste site. The city sent inspectors to investigate who reported even more hazardous conditions than simply black ooze in basements. The inspectors found large holes in the surface of the covered canal presumably caused by collapsing waste barrels under the ground. They discovered that chemical residues remained on the surface of the canal after rainwater had evaporated. The city's solution was to cover the holes with dirt.

In the 1970s residents reported that the strong chemical odors coming from the landfill site were much worse after a heavy rain. Puddles of rainwater took days to evaporate. More and more residents began to find the thick black ooze on their basement walls and floors. Grass, flowers, and trees in backyards withered and died. Huge holes appeared in yards for no apparent reason.

In 1976 a joint U.S.-Canadian commission identified traces of an insecticide in Lake Ontario fish and began an investigation that traced the source of the insecticide to a dump site near Love Canal used by Hooker Chemicals. The media picked up on the story, and residents, many of them for the very first time, heard the history of Love Canal. They read of William Love's dream of an industrial community, the excavation of the canal, and its purchase by Hooker Chemicals as a waste disposal site. They read of the company's "gift" of the toxic site to the city and the city's subsequent construction of an elementary school on top of the chemical dump. And they read of increasing complaints by residents that something was wrong in their community. An enterprising journalist secretly took a sample of the black oily substance found in so many residents' basements and had it privately analyzed. He discovered—and publicized—that the ooze contained toxic materials, traced to Hooker Chemicals.

Early in 1977 the city of Niagara Falls hired a consulting company to develop a program that would reduce persistent groundwater pollution in the area. The consulting company's subsequent report to the city indicated that a majority of the homeowners at the southern end of the landfill were plagued with chemical residues and strong odors in their basements. The report further claimed that storm sewers west of the landfill contained PCB (polychlorinated biphenyl). In several areas of the canal, it was found, corroded waste drums were within 3 feet of the surface, and in some places waste drums actually protruded from the ground, exposed to the air. The consulting company's report recommended that the city clean up the landfill site and offered a plan for doing so that would cost $425,000. City officials, comparing the large price tag of the plan with their meager city budget, did not adopt the proposal.

The consulting company's report and the city's rejection of its cleanup proposal were well publicized in newspaper articles and editorials. Incensed, one city resident contacted his congressional representative, who subsequently visited the Love Canal area in September 1977. The congressman urged the city manager to adopt the proposal for cleanup but in vain. Meanwhile, tests on the contents of the landfill were being conducted by the New York State Health Department. In the summer of 1978, the Health Department reported that the results of their tests indicated that more than 200 chemicals had been dumped in the landfill. A significant number of the chemicals were either known to be carcinogenic or suspected of being so. Health hazards associated with exposure to the chemicals identified in the dump site range from convulsions, skin irritation, anemia, deafness, and visual defects to liver damage, hepatitis, renal damage, acute leukemia, and respiratory arrest.

Based on the test results, the state health commissioner strongly urged the county Health Department to take actions to reduce the serious health and welfare threats that the toxic conditions at Love Canal posed to residents. The county Health Department also drew on a limited budget, however, and so county officials responded with band-aid measures, placing dirt on the exposed waste drums and fencing off one area of the canal site to keep people out. For off-site problems, the county provided electric fans so that residents could ventilate their basements.

Alarmed residents began to speak with one another about the landfill and found that they shared concerns about health and property. They spoke with reporters, and news coverage increased. The subsequent pressure on elected officials, particularly in this gubernatorial election year, provoked public meetings about the landfill. Concerned citizens were able to identify each other and were quite vocal at the public meetings in berating various public officials.

State officials stepped in and convened a special meeting in the summer of 1978 specifically to convey information to the public and gain their cooperation. The special meeting was intended to calm residents' fears and assure them that appropriate steps were being taken to protect them. Instead, the meeting became a basis for mobilizing and uniting residents who were concerned about the toxic effects of the landfill. Residents' refusal to be reassured of their safety brought state agencies into the fray, and these agencies subsequently assumed major responsibility for the Love Canal problem. This effectively eliminated any significant role for the city government in the toxic drama.

During the summer of 1978, residents became more alarmed about the effects of the chemical waste dump and the lack of action to protect residents. Several citizens groups emerged to engage in grassroots environmental conflict. One short-lived group was organized by a woman who had suffered property damage, which she attributed to poisons leaching from the landfill and killing plants. In 1974 her in-ground swimming pool had risen 2 feet out of the ground from the pressures of underground water. After the swimming pool was removed, the hole soon filled with chemical-laden water. The vegetation in her backyard withered and died. In the summer of 1978, the homeowner collected signatures on a petition for relief from property taxes for those homeowners whose property had been damaged because of the landfill.

The largest, most formally organized, and most enduring citizens organization was initiated by Lois Gibbs. Her son developed severe asthmatic symptoms and convulsions when he attended the elementary school on the landfill site. The newspaper articles of that summer of 1978 convinced Gibbs that her son's illnesses were linked to the landfill. Armed with letters from physicians, she requested that the school board transfer her son to another school for health reasons. When the school board flatly rejected her request, she was determined to form a committee of like-minded residents to demand that the school area either be cleaned up or closed down.

To enlist support from neighborhood residents, Gibbs went door-to-door for weeks and found many residents who shared her feelings, opinions, and fears about the landfill. Mothers repeatedly described to Gibbs the same birth defects and illnesses in their children. Organizing these concerned citizens, Gibbs forged the Love Canal Homeowners Committee (later the Love Canal Homeowners Association, the LCHA), with three goals: to obtain restitution for property losses; to clean up the chemical landfill; and to close the elementary school on the landfill site.

The citizens organization had about 100 members when the state announced it would sponsor a public meeting on the Love Canal landfill site in Albany on August 2, 1978. At the meeting, the New York State health commissioner was scheduled to deliver an announcement about the landfill. Several LCHA leaders attended the meeting, fully expecting to be encouraged to take part in discussions about what would be done to protect residents. Instead, the leaders were presented with a stark, alarming pronouncement. The health commissioner said that the landfill "constitutes a public nuisance and an extremely serious threat and danger to the health, safety, and welfare of residents" (Levine 1982:28). He officially declared the existence of an emergency and ordered the city of Niagara Falls to stop the migration of the chemicals from the landfill site and to undertake studies on the extent of chronic diseases of residents living near the site. Furthermore, he recommended that residents avoid their basements and not eat the food from their gardens. Most terrifying, he urged the families of pregnant women and children under two years of age to relocate temporarily as soon as possible.

The public announcement received massive international media coverage. "Love Canal" quickly became a symbol of the negative side of industrialism. Within days, President Jimmy Carter declared a state emergency at Love Canal. He also announced his backing of an amendment that would allocate $4 million in federal money to the cleanup of the canal site. New York Governor Hugh Carey responded with a promise that the state would buy private homes bordering the canal, but there was a proviso: the state would only buy the homes of those residents who could demonstrate health disorders in their families that were directly related to the materials in the Love Canal.

The health commissioner's public pronouncement of the dump site as a serious danger was a powerful mobilizing event for Love Canal residents. Levine writes that, with the commissioner's statement, "the spark was lit that inflamed an already heated community" (1982:175). As they were informed of the history of Love Canal, residents came to understand that corporate and government decisions made much earlier based on economic returns had led to the poisoning of their community, their properties, their homes, and their very bodies. Simultaneously with the commissioner's statement, city officials closed the elementary school on the waste site, but this victory seemed hollow in the face of the grave public announcement that heightened residents' fears.

In addition, many residents were angered both by the governor's limited offer to buy some homes and by the planned cleanup project at the canal site, which, many believed, was remedial at best and dangerous at worst. The governor's plan provided for the evacuation and state purchase of only those homes in the innermost concentric ring around the canal site. The cleanup project called for stopping the leaching of chemicals from the site and for covering up the canal. Residents objected that little was known or had even been studied about the migration of leaching chemicals. Many argued that the state's assumption that leaching occurred uniformly in all directions from the site might be completely inaccurate.

Two days after the health commissioner's announcement and warnings, the Love Canal Homeowners Committee became the Love Canal Homeowners Association (LCHA), and members conducted their first meeting with several hundred in attendance. They hired an attorney who immediately raised the issue of the lack of safety features in the proposed cleanup project. Residents feared that work at the waste disposal site would release toxic chemical fumes or cause an explosion or fire; only a hundred yards away people would continue to go about their daily lives. Residents advocated the permanent relocation of residents living closest to the canal site.

Gibbs led the organization as its president. New York State provided office space in the now-closed elementary school building and for two years paid utility, telephone, and some general expenses for the group. For strategical planning, Gibbs consulted her brother-in-law, a biologist and faculty member of SUNY-Buffalo with previous environmental protest experience. He suggested how to handle the media and described the governmental structure in which Gibbs would have to work. He also offered some basic points on organizing people and introduced her to other environmentalists who supported the LCHA throughout the battle.

The core activists in LCHA were chiefly female homemakers who gradually educated themselves and each other about toxic chemicals, waste disposal laws, and political processes. Money for the group was raised by various kinds of fund-raisers, membership fees ($1 per family), and donations. Activists conducted health surveys and made public speeches. They marched on City Hall, picketed the cleanup site, and burned in effigy the governor and the state health commissioner.

Hooker Chemicals' moves were defensive. Corporate officials insisted that it was unfair to blame Hooker for the disaster. After all, they argued, Hooker had clearly warned the city of Niagara Falls of possible adverse effects from the chemical wastes in their disclaimer in the deed of sale when they sold the property to the city for $1. As an example of self-described corporate good citizenship, Hooker Chemicals employees developed an on-site safety plan for the cleanup project. Residents and LCHA members were opposed to the cleanup plan, which lacked adequate safety provisions for residents off-site. They rejected a proposed off-site emergency evacuation plan as being hopelessly inadequate. Members argued that, by the time a person was notified of an emergency, much of the damage would already have been done.

Nor were city and county government officials satisfactorily responsive to residents' needs. The economic base of Niagara Falls was already deteriorating at the time of the health commissioner's announcement. The city budget simply had no room for the more than $20 million that would be necessary for the relocation and cleanup project unless federal funding was provided. At the same time, Hooker Chemicals' officials were in the process of choosing a community as the site for the construction of their new corporate headquarters. The selected community would experience a significant boon to the local economy. The city of Niagara Falls was currently in the running for this economic prize.

LCHA members had lost faith in city and county agencies and turned hopefully to the state, to Governor Carey and officials of the State Department of Health. The governor was sympathetic in his statements to residents and to the press, at least prior to that year's primary elections. The Department of Health conducted a health survey using questionnaires and blood tests. However, LCHA members and other residents complained that the questionnaires were confusing and did not even focus on their main concern: children's health. The blood testing was done so erratically and the results were distributed so rarely that residents benefited very little from the state's efforts.

Consequently, residents conducted their own health survey, testing their hypothesis that leaking substances were not migrating uniformly in all directions from the site. Residents could distribute the questionnaires for the health survey, but because they could not analyze the data themselves, they sent the completed questionnaires to the laboratories of the State Department of Health for analysis. When they never received full reports from the state laboratories analyzing the data they collected, residents felt that both scientists and officials had ignored their need for information.

Residents like Gibbs who lived outside the innermost ring of homes slated for temporary relocation were concerned that the effects of the leaking landfill were not confined to such human-defined boundaries. They were also fearful that harmful effects from the cleanup process would not stop at those same boundaries but would cross the neighborhoods whose families had been evacuated and reach families in the outer rings. In October 1978 the state health commissioner refused to relocate families in the outer ring homes during cleanup work; residents felt betrayed at all levels of government. Levine describes the residents' feelings: "This episode marked a significant point in the people's growing mistrust of the intentions of the state. At first, the people, long accustomed to what they viewed as indifference or worse from the city and county officials they encountered, had wanted to trust all the state experts who had become visible on the scene in the spring of 1978, seemingly ready and eager to help. The people's trust faded step by step; first they began to mistrust the lower-level workers, then the elected politicians and high-level appointed officials" (1982:68–69).

As the residents' concerns increased, they pressed for the *permanent* relocation of families living in the inner and some of the outer rings around the canal site. They were again rebuffed in February 1979. In a public meeting the following August, the state health commissioner reported that dioxins had been found in the Love Canal landfill. Although some dioxins are among the most deadly substances known, the commissioner repeated his assertion of no more relocations. To the further outrage of many residents, he advised families contemplating pregnancy that, since they had been dutifully informed of the dangers from the toxic site, any medical problems arising during pregnancy or childhood would be due to their own decision.

Litigation loomed everywhere. New York State filed suit against Hooker Chemicals. Hooker Chemicals filed countersuits against New York State, the city of Niagara Falls, the Niagara County Board of Education, and the Niagara County Health Department. In the spring of 1979, Hooker Chemicals held a press conference in which company officials distributed written statements. Hooker took out full-page newspaper advertisements and distributed colorful brochures that emphasized the company's concern for Love Canal residents, reminded residents of the company's economic importance as a local employer, and praised themselves for their adherence to state-of-the-art waste disposal methods.

In December 1979 the U.S. Justice Department filed suit on behalf of the Environmental Protection Agency (EPA) against Hooker Chemicals. The EPA ordered that a pilot sample of thirty-six residents be tested for chromosomal damage. When data analysis and the report were completed in May 1980, the results revealed that eleven of the thirty-six people who had been tested did indeed have chromosomal damage. The EPA had not intended to publicize the report until they had the findings reviewed, but the report was leaked to the *New York Times* and the *Buffalo Courier Express*. Within hours, newspaper headlines all over the world announced the findings of chromosomal damage at Love Canal. The LCHA received telephone inquiries about the findings from all over the United States and several foreign countries.

The EPA issued a press release saying that the study was being reviewed for the accuracy of the findings. Agency officials stated that, if the review confirmed the findings, they would make a decision as to whether the new evidence would justify a recommendation for the temporary relocation of Love Canal residents in the outer ring of homes around the landfill site. The announcement also alluded to the possibility of a later, more comprehensive survey of chromosomal damage, if warranted.

On May 17, 1980, two days after the group of thirty-six residents had been told the results of their chromosome tests, a crowd gathered outside LCHA headquarters. A few waited for the results of yet another test. Others wanted to know what would happen next—would there be more chromosome testing? Other kinds of health studies? Should they have another child? What should they tell their married children? They waited to address their questions to two EPA officials from the Washington office who had remained in Niagara Falls to answer questions. By the time the officials arrived in late afternoon, a crowd of about fifty angry people, mostly women and their children, had gathered outside LCHA headquarters.

Gibbs informed the EPA officials that they were to be detained in the headquarters to protect them from the angry crowd. The crowd urged that the officials be held until word came from Washington that Love Canal people would be moved out. Gibbs called the White House and told the switchboard operator, "We are holding two EPA officials hostage" (Levine 1982:149). The EPA officials remained in the headquarters for about five hours, after which they were released into a crowd of about 125. The next day the officials were recalled to Washington, and the women most involved in the episode were severely reprimanded by EPA administrators.

On May 21, before the EPA's review of the chromosome study had been completed, the agency issued a press release announcing the decision that the federal government would *temporarily* relocate about 700 outer ring families exposed to the toxic wastes deposited in the canal by Hooker Chemicals. The press release noted that the government's suit against Hooker would be amended to include reimbursement for the costs of relocation. Although Love Canal residents were somewhat relieved, many still wanted permanent rather than temporary relocation.

In August 1980, a presidential election year, President Jimmy Carter authorized an agreement for the federal government to purchase Love Canal residents' homes in the outer ring. By 1987 the Love Canal community was virtually abandoned. To this day, no systematic health surveys have been conducted to assess the health effects of living near the waste disposal site; no geological studies have been done to identify the migration routes of the leaching toxic chemicals; and no permanent solution has been implemented to assure the containment of the chemical wastes. Recently, the federal government pronounced the area safe and authorized the selling of the Love Canal homes purchased from residents in the relocation effort. Those most interested in buying low-priced, "formerly" contaminated homes tend to be young couples planning to start a family or families with preschool children.

The uncanny fear and dread precipitated by developments at Love Canal might have subsided and the specter of Love Canal might not have become an international symbol of the new species of trouble, if Three Mile Island had never happened. Three Mile Island is the site of the worst commercial nuclear power accident in U.S. history. The incident began on March 28, 1979, less than a year after the "grave and imminent peril" pronouncement at Love Canal. For the residents of many communities across the country which hosted some type of facility with noxious effects for the environment, *one* human-made environmental disaster is an accident but *two* such disasters suggest a pattern.

Three Mile Island

The Three Mile Island (TMI) nuclear power station is located on a long, narrow island in the Susquehanna River in southcentral Pennsylvania. Except for moderate urban and industrial centers in Lancaster and the state capital of Harrisburg, the area consists of a network of small towns, farms, and rural communities stretching along the scenic Susquehanna River just prior to its discharge into the Chesapeake Bay. About 38,000 people live in a 5-mile radius of the TMI nuclear power plant and 600,000 in a 20-mile radius. The majority of the population of southcentral Pennsylvania is white, working class, and politically conservative.

When plans for the nuclear power plant were proposed in the late 1960s, most area residents were either neutral toward the proposal or regarded it favorably. A large Air Force base in the area had recently closed, and many citizens welcomed the power plant for its potential employment opportunities and business revenues that might compensate for the closing of the military base.

The first reactor built on the island, Unit 1, began commercial operation in 1974. A second reactor, Unit 2, was proposed in 1977 when the oil cartel's virtual control of oil prices led many to view nuclear energy as more important than ever for decreasing U.S. dependence on foreign oil imports. Unit 2 began testing using nuclear fuel in March 1978. The reactor experienced numerous technical problems throughout the year of testing. Despite such problems, the Nuclear Regulatory Commission (NRC) granted the utility company permission to begin commercial service at Unit 2. Unit 2 was brought on line on December 31, 1978, just in time for the utility company to qualify for $35 million in federal investment tax credits and $20 million in depreciation writeoffs for the tax year of 1978.

On Wednesday, March 28, 1979, merely three months after beginning commercial operations, TMI's Unit 2 reactor suffered a severe loss-of-coolant accident. Unknown amounts of radioactive steam were unintentionally released into the atmosphere. This was the first stage in what became a partial meltdown of the reactor core. An internal "general emergency" was issued. The 7:00 A.M. shift reported, but workers were not permitted on the island. Consequently, they knew something had gone wrong. Most area residents did not know of the continuing crisis or its seriousness until Thursday evening. On Thursday the media reported that things at TMI were under control. Although radiation still leaked unintentionally into the atmosphere, officials from federal and local agencies and from the utility company insisted that the leakages posed no serious health hazard to the public. But many residents suspected that they were not being told the whole truth.

On Friday morning an especially large and uncontrolled release of radioactivity spewed into the atmosphere. The Pennsylvania State Police went door-to-door in the communities within 10 miles of the plant and advised residents to remain indoors with their windows closed and their air conditioning units turned off until noon. Pennsylvania Governor Richard Thornburg, who was later appointed by President George Bush as U.S. attorney general, issued an evacuation advisory, a somewhat milder warning than an evacuation order, to pregnant women and preschool children living within 5 miles of the plant.

The governor's evacuation advisory prompted a large segment of the nonpregnant population without preschoolers to leave the area. Families scattered to motels and to relatives' homes, regretting the haste that led them to flee without family photographs or other mementos. Many left believing they would never see their homes again, that the area would be destroyed and uninhabitable. A number of families experienced serious conflict deciding whether or not to evacuate. Some people whose occupations entailed service to the public during emergencies suffered role strain in trying to determine which allegiance was more binding, family or occupation (Walsh 1981).

Estimates of the percentage of the population that evacuated the area within a 15-mile radius of the TMI plant range from 39 percent to 52 percent. The heaviest evacuation occurred on Friday, March 30, but families continued to leave home throughout the weekend. On Sunday, President Jimmy Carter and Governor Thornburg visited the plant, but their visit did little to reassure evacuees, most of whom stayed away from the area a week or more.

The crisis at the Unit 2 reactor continued for two weeks, as off-site releases of radiation occurred and temperatures in the reactor core remained dangerously high. Residents were repeatedly assured by the utility company and by the federal government's regulatory agency, the NRC, that the plant was safe. Only over the next few years was the seriousness of the accident more accurately assessed and publicized. Residents later learned that: Unit 2 had been within thirty to sixty minutes of a core meltdown; it was unlikely that anyone would ever know exactly how much radiation escaped at Unit 2 because the radiation levels exceeded the capacities of the plant instruments to measure them; and utility officials had not given the NRC complete information on the severity of the accident as it occurred.

Evacuees returned to their homes but found that their ordeal was far from over. They were confronted with further problems associated with the severely damaged and still dangerous Unit 2 reactor. The accident required a massive cleanup operation that had never before been undertaken in the nuclear industry. To that point, no nuclear reactor had ever been decommissioned, that is, taken out of service. Consequently, the appropriate technology for the cleanup of Unit 2 was not apparent, even among experts.

Returning evacuees also had to deal with the utility company's determination to restart Unit 1, the undamaged nuclear reactor. It had coincidentally been shut down for routine refueling at the time of the Unit 2 accident. Many residents were concerned at the thought of Unit 1 being operated by the same utility company that may have been responsible for the Unit 2 accident. They also feared the consequences of putting Unit 1 in operation only a few yards away from the still unstable Unit 2.

Residents gathered information about the accident in Unit 2 and the proposed restart of Unit 1 through extensive coverage by the media that was generally critical of the utility company and the nuclear industry. Community leaders criticized the utility company in public interviews. Neighbors conversed in backyards and over the telephone, sharing their fears. A strong opposition to the restart of Unit 1 emerged and grew. This opposition was the basis for the founding of several citizens organizations to engage in a grassroots conflict to ban the restart.

Efforts to mobilize citizens organizations were substantially aided by frequent rallies and hearings in the TMI area. About 95 percent of those people who later became active in a grassroots organization reported attending at least one rally or hearing (Walsh 1988:58). The first major rally was held on April 6, 1979, in Harrisburg, and about 1000 persons attended, a turnout assessed as good since many evacuees had not yet returned to their homes. In May 1979 the President's Commission on the Accident at Three Mile Island began public hearings, which offered residents important opportunities to vocalize their fears and anger and to hear their neighbors voicing similar concerns.

Activists in national antinuclear organizations recognized that the TMI accident would give the larger antinuclear movement increased credibility, for it had confirmed these activists' fears and given legitimacy to their concerns. Therefore, they quickly organized a national antinuclear rally in Washington, D.C., on May 6 in support of TMI residents; attendance was estimated at over 120,000. Thirty busloads of TMI area residents were accorded places of honor at the march and rally as the most recent victims of nuclear power. Speakers at the rally emphasized the importance of preventing the restart of Unit 1 and viewed success in banning the restart as a potentially critical step in breaking the nuclear industry. TMI-area residents came away from the rally appreciating this national support and newly aware of the long struggle with the nuclear industry that lay before them.

Within two months of the accident, several grassroots environmental organizations had emerged to exert pressure on local governmental bodies to take a public stand opposing the Unit 1 restart. The groups claimed partial credit for the passage of at least ten anti-restart resolutions passed by borough or township governments within six months of the accident. Five of the resolutions demanded that certain safety conditions be met before allowing Unit 1 to restart, and the other five demanded that the plant be permanently closed as a nuclear facility. In contrast, only one pro-restart resolution was passed. None of the resolutions was legally binding, but they indicated the strength of opposition to the restart.

The grassroots groups also urged the governor to oppose a restart, at least until the NRC held public hearings to determine the conditions under which Unit 1 could safely be operated. The governor responded in June 1979 by writing to the NRC, expressing his strong opposition to the restart until serious safety issues could be resolved and suggesting that the Commonwealth of Pennsylvania might pursue legal recourse in the event the agency gave an immediate restart order.

In August 1979 the NRC ordered that Unit 1 be closed indefinitely, until the completion of formal adjudicatory hearings to determine whether there was reasonable assurance that Unit 1 could be operated without endangering the public's health and safety. *Adjudicatory hearings* are formal proceedings in which involved parties may present oral testimony, cross-examine opposing witnesses, and have their cases directed by attorneys. Consequently, the NRC hearings permitted considerable participation by members of the grassroots organizations opposed to the Unit 1 restart.

The NRC created a special panel, the Atomic Safety and Licensing Board, to preside over the hearings on the restart of the Unit 1 reactor. As required by law, the agency gave notice of the opportunity for public participation in the hearings. The hearings were originally scheduled to begin in the spring of 1980, but were delayed until the following October because of the large number of issues raised in prehearings. Many of those issues had been brought before the public by the grassroots organizations. For example, some members expressed concern regarding the psychological stress on residents that the restart would pose. Others insisted that the integrity and competence of the managers of the utility company be scrutinized.

By ordering restart hearings prior to its decision on a Unit 1 restart, the NRC imposed an important constraint on the groups' choice of strategies. Activists were legally bound to go through the NRC in fighting a restart; they could not appeal directly to civil courts. Most activists never seriously doubted that the NRC would eventually vote in favor of the Unit 1 restart, given the mutually supportive relationship they had already observed between the regulators and the regulated. Rather, they hoped to win in the civil courts. To apply to the courts, however, they had first to remain intact through the process of arguing their contentions against the restart in the adjudicatory hearings. To be formal intervenors in the restart hearings required technical and legal expertise. Consequently, the grassroots groups were forced to adopt a litigation strategy, in addition to their other strategies.

With the opening of the restart hearings in October 1980, most of the grassroots groups focused their efforts and resources on their arguments against the restart. Issues raised in the hearings included: plant design/ hardware; emergency evacuation planning; the utility company's financial capability and management competence to operate Unit 1; and the psychological stress that a Unit 1 restart would likely induce among residents.

Although the hearings ended in July 1981, no restart decision by the NRC commissioners was forthcoming. The restart decision was first delayed by the so-called cheating scandal which emerged in August 1981 and consisted of charges that TMI control room operators had cheated on a licensing examination with the full knowledge and consent of some supervisory personnel. Eventually, the issue was resolved by simply retesting the operators. Also delaying a decision was the unexpected discovery in 1981 of thousands of leaking steam generator tubes in the Unit 1 reactor. The discovery heightened fears about the safety of operating Unit 1. The restart decision was further delayed by an appeals court decision in January 1982 that ruled against the NRC and required the agency to do a time-consuming environmental assessment on the psychological stress likely to be generated by the restart of Unit 1.

Such events maintained and increased opposition to the restart among area residents. That their opposition had not appreciably diminished in three years' time was amply demonstrated in a May 1982 nonbinding referendum in which residents voted two to one against the Unit 1 restart.

In late 1983 a federal grand jury in Harrisburg indicted the utility company on eleven charges of criminally falsifying test data on coolant leaks and destroying documents prior to the Unit 2 accident. Many experts believed that such falsifications had obscured the actual conditions during the Unit 2 accident and made it more difficult to control the runaway reactor. Several months later, the NRC commissioners voted three to two to separate management integrity issues from their decision on the Unit 1 restart. The utility company immediately pleaded guilty to one count and no contest to six others in a criminal court plea bargain. It agreed to pay $1 million to an emergency planning fund and received a $45,000 fine. In August 1984 Governor Thornburg urged the NRC not to vote on the restart until hearings were concluded on funding for the Unit 2 cleanup. In February 1985, however, the NRC voted that no further hearings were needed before the restart decision.

Even though local officials, the state governor, and U.S. senators all supported the grassroots groups' cause, demanding that the NRC hold further hearings to address serious doubts about the utility's competence, the NRC voted in May 1985 to allow the Unit 1 restart. The decision marked "the beginning of the most organized and widespread civil disobedience in the whole struggle" (Walsh 1988:167). Within hours of the NRC decision, about 250 protestors blocked the gates of the TMI plant, approximately 82 of whom were arrested for refusing a police order to leave. A two-hour protest march was carried out without violence or injuries.

The restart issue went from the streets to the courts. Governor Thornburg, on behalf of the commonwealth, petitioned the federal Third Circuit Court of Appeals to nullify the NRC's decision to permit the restart. The appeal concerned the need for further hearings before any decision about a Unit 1 restart. The court temporarily halted the restart and agreed to hear arguments on the need for further Unit 1 management integrity hearings. In September 1985, however, the federal court voted ten to two against further review of the restart case, clearing the way for a September 25 restart.

Supreme Court Justice William J. Brennan ordered a stay of the restart while awaiting the full court's decision regarding a review of the case. On October 2, 1985, the U.S. Supreme Court voted eight to one against hearing the Unit 1 case and lifted the stay. Unit 1 was restarted the very next day. Permission to restart Unit 1 in the face of such strong and widespread opposition, even among regional political elites, gives some indication of the tremendous power wielded by corporations, in the form of the nuclear industry, and the federal government. It also suggests the fragility of democratic procedures in the face of economic concerns.

SUMMARY

In neither of these cases of grassroots environmental conflict did the citizens organizations succeed in having their environmental problems completely resolved. Love Canal residents who were relocated when the federal government bought their homes still wait, still anxiously watch their children for any sign of illness, still live with the dread. TMI-area residents realize they will never know the extent of their exposure, realize that one ear will always be tuned to the alarm bells on the island, and realize that the "uncanny fear" will be with them always.

Perhaps we should adjust our notion of the "outcomes" of grassroots environmental organizations and avoid evaluating them as either successful or unsuccessful solely on the basis of their stated goals. Perhaps there is more to success than removing every vestige of environmental harm, which is impossible anyway. In both communities, many residents underwent a profound change in worldview and political consciousness. In fact, Lois Gibbs left Love Canal and moved to Washington, D.C., to found the Citizens Clearinghouse on Hazardous Wastes, an environmental organization through which activists have established nationwide networks of community groups that wage grassroots environmental battles over toxic wastes. This change in consciousness, this disillusionment with the political system, is a powerful force for social change. Activists at Love Canal and at TMI discovered that the system did not necessarily work for them. They found that democratic processes cannot be taken for granted—they must be demanded again and again.

7. *The Breaking of the Faith*

Public concern about environmental quality was awakened with the revelations at Love Canal and the dread at TMI. The national environmental organizations might have been able to use heightened public fears to launch another round of protective legislation had they not immediately encountered the intense deregulatory mood of the Reagan administration. For several years after Reagan took office, the economy was in a state of decline. To bolster the weak economy—and because the administration was strongly driven by ideology—the government became more closely allied with capitalist interests than had been characteristic of preceding administrations. Officials who supported the increase of economic growth targeted many federal environmental regulations for elimination. The environmental deregulation policies of the Reagan administration, together with continuing discoveries of contaminated working-class communities in the 1980s, led to substantial increases in public support for environmental protection (Dunlap and Scarce 1991).

In this chapter, we discuss the concurrent trends of decreasing environmental regulation and increasing environmental contamination that characterized the 1980s and draw out their implications for social class issues.

ENVIRONMENTAL DEREGULATION

Piven and Cloward describe the actions of Reagan's administration as a renewal of social class conflict: "In the aftermath of the election of 1980, the Reagan administration and its big-business allies declared a new class war on the unemployed, the unemployable, and the working poor" (1982:1). The new class war was manifested in the reduction of numerous social programs. Piven and Cloward argue that social programs were cut as part of the Reagan administration's larger strategy to increase business profits in order to stimulate the economy. The administration and its supporters claimed that greater profits for corporations would lead to greater prosperity for all through the investment, entrepreneurial effort, and innovation that combine to produce more jobs and rising income for everyone in the society. Reagan's administration became the voice of the corporate class, arguing that the weak economy was due to the undermining of American industry's economic dominance in the world. The undercutting had been perpetrated by the federal government itself, it was argued, by tampering with the delicate market mechanism through increases in taxes, government spending—especially on social programs that artificially inflate the cost of labor—and regulatory action.

To counter those effects, the Reagan administration mounted a three-pronged effort to stimulate corporate profits. The plan called for federal tax cuts for business, the relaxation of regulatory activities, and a substantially increased military budget.

Since the corporate class consistently argued that high taxes on large businesses and the wealthy reduce profitability and discourage investment, one measure to stimulate the economy was tax reduction. Consequently, under Reagan the federal tax structure was reorganized so that changes in laws governing investment and depreciation writeoffs favored large corporations over small businesses. In addition, personal income and estate taxes were significantly reduced for those with annual incomes exceeding $50,000.

A second measure was to reduce regulation. Industry was saved billions of dollars "by undoing the apparatus through which government regulates business" (Piven and Cloward 1982:7). During his presidential campaign Reagan had said, "There are tens of thousands of regulations I'd like to see eliminated" (Lash 1984:xii). His view was compatible with the corporate class's argument that government regulations shrink profits by increasing the costs of doing business and inhibiting entrepreneurial innovation. The Reagan administration cut the budgets and reduced the power of the federal regulatory agencies, including those that regulated industrial pollution, workplace health and safety standards, equal opportunities for women and minorities in hiring, antitrust suits, and the exploitation of mineral resources on federal lands.

In a third measure intended to increase corporate profits and boost the sagging economy, Reagan increased the military budget. Consistent with Reagan's views of the need to protect the United States from "the evil empire," the Soviet Union, the administration hiked the military budget to unprecedented peacetime levels. Since military production activities are carried out by private corporate contractors, the more dollars allocated to the military, the greater the financial benefits to various large defense industries such as General Dynamics and Lockheed and to their suppliers.

The Reagan administration's efforts did, as intended, increase corporate profits. The result of these policy changes affecting the tax structure, the regulation of industry, and the military budget was a massive upward redistribution of wealth. The rich got richer, and the gap between the top and the bottom of the income scale became greater and more obvious: the new class war was enjoined.

A particular Reagan target and consequently one of the casualties of the new class war was environmental regulation. Defended in terms of the need for less government bureaucracy and fewer impediments to profit, the Reagan administration's successful attacks on existing and proposed environmental regulations signaled the strong resurgence of corporate power. The importance Reagan attached to environmental deregulation was apparent in his appointment of Vice-President George Bush to chair the Task Force on Regulatory Relief. In his book *A Season of Spoils* (1984), Jonathan Lash describes how the Reagan administration systematically weakened environmental protection and the enforcement of existing laws in order to remove the obstacles that environmental regulations allegedly placed in corporate paths to profits. Reagan's war on the environment was waged through two major attacks: the virtual dismantling of the EPA enforcement office, and the premeditated neglect of the Superfund program.

The EPA was established in 1970 with responsibility for monitoring corporate production activities and assuring their compliance with environmental law. The EPA enforcement office operates through ten regional offices that have the power to inspect facilities, to hold hearings in which officials determine whether environmental laws have been violated, and to levy fines for noncompliance with the laws. The EPA cannot, however, take companies to court for noncompliance. If a firm continues to violate environmental standards, the EPA regional office has the option to send the case for review to EPA headquarters in Washington, D.C., where administrators decide whether to refer the case to the U.S. Department of Justice. The decision to prosecute the corporate violator is made solely within the Justice Department.

The Reagan administration appointed Anne Gorsuch as head of the EPA. Like Reagan, she believed that EPA enforcement had been overzealous in the past, and she reorganized the agency in a way that nearly eliminated the enforcement office. The former staff of 2100 was scattered across the agency into various program offices, and the enforcement office was left with Enforcement Counsel William Sullivan and a skeleton staff (Lash 1984). Following Gorsuch's lead, Sullivan instructed the administrators of EPA's ten regional offices not to send cases of persistent corporate violators to headquarters without first exhausting every opportunity for settlement. According to Lash's interview with Sullivan, Sullivan told the administrators of the regional offices, "Every case you do refer will be a black mark against you" (Lash 1984:47). Evidence for the change in enforcement policy is apparent in the numbers: in 1980, under Carter's presidency, the regional offices had referred 313 cases of persistent corporate violators to headquarters; in 1981, after Gorsuch's appointment, only 59 cases were referred.

The Reagan administration's second major attack on environmental protection was through neglect of the Superfund program. The revelations at Love Canal had led to the 1980 passage of the Comprehensive Environmental Response, Compensation and Liability Act (CERCLA) that created the $1.6 billion, five-year Superfund for the cleanup of hazardous wastes. The purpose of the Superfund program was to prepare for future Love Canals, since it was well known that the thousands of abandoned hazardous waste dumps across the nation were likely to affect nearby communities through contamination of water, soil, and air.

CERCLA mandated that the EPA would pay for the cleanup of hazardous waste sites designated as severe hazards and placed on the National Priority List. The agency would then sue the responsible parties to recover the cleanup costs, with the ultimate intent of revoking the corporate right to externalize the environmental costs of production. Superfund money was provided in large part by chemical industries through a special tax, which, at least temporarily, allowed industrywide externalization. The tax on chemical industries amounted to about $280 million per year, less than one-fifth of 1 percent of the chemical industry's annual sales (Lash 1984). CERCLA provided for the special tax only for the five years of the Superfund program.

In the first two and one-half years of the Superfund program, cleanup had been completed at only 5 of 419 waste sites on the priority list. Only one-quarter of the fund had been used, and the time allotted by Congress for the administration of the program was half over. A congressional vote would be required to reenact the tax on chemical industries and extend the Superfund program beyond 1985. Congressional hearings on delays in the cleanup program revealed that the Reagan administration was deliberately holding back on the Superfund program. At a Senate Committee on Environment and Public Works hearing, both the director of the Superfund program and the EPA head of enforcement for hazardous wastes answered "yes" to the following question posed by a senator: "Was there any policy explicitly or implicitly to slow down expenditures from the Superfund so that there would be money left in the fund when the law expires in order to support the preconceived notion that no extension of the law was necessary and to minimize the problem" (Lash 1984:91)?

In a later hearing before a House of Representatives subcommittee, the director of the Superfund program testified, "There was a hidden agenda, if you will, not to set in motion events that would lead to what is referred to as 'Son of Superfund' or the extension of the tax on reenactment of the law beyond the 1985 cutoff" (Lash 1984:90).

A year after the Superfund's initial funding ended, Congress in 1986 passed the Superfund Amendments and Reauthorization Act (SARA), which increased the program's funding to $9 billion over the next five years and imposed several regulations to help ensure that the program would meet its objectives.

SARA had only minimal effect. Again, the corporate state structure operated to protect the expansion of industrial production. An important requirement of SARA was the stipulation that the cleanup technologies used would guarantee the permanent reduction of the amount, toxicity, and mobility of hazardous wastes to the maximum extent possible. But in 1987 a study indicated that only twenty-five of the seventy-four final cleanup plans approved by the EPA since 1986 had followed SARA's mandate for permanent treatment technologies. Another SARA requirement is uniformity of cleanup standards, but such standards have not been issued, allowing industries a loophole to appeal cleanup plans proposed for their sites. SARA also required that EPA make funds available for residents of contaminated communities to hire independent consultants to evaluate EPA's cleanup plan. Before the grant program had been fully installed, however, EPA spent sixteen months writing regulations for the grants; in the meantime, seventy-five final cleanup plans were approved without community input (Feagin and Feagin 1990).

Why did the Reagan administration shelve the Superfund program? The reasons were both political and ideological. Indeed, the two are difficult to separate, since the administration received major campaign financing from the corporations that had the most to lose, both in taxes and the potentially much larger lawsuit settlements, should the Superfund be extended and/or pursue its mandate vigorously. Although Superfund administrators consistently tried to use announcements of Superfund sites to benefit Republican election campaigns and to avoid benefiting Democratic candidates (Lash 1984), corporate support was far more crucial to them. The ideological component was consistent with Reagan's overall economic plans: the Superfund program was to be ended in order to keep social spending down and to relieve the chemical industry of the growth-deadening burden of assuming financial responsibility for the social and environmental costs of production.

Federal funds are often allocated on the basis of party politics, for example, the distribution of federal money for highways, dams, and new buildings is routinely affected by politics. However, withholding federal funds allocated for the cleanup of hazardous waste sites has a more serious effect than the inconvenience of an old highway or an aging building. Reagan's policy of the planned neglect of hazardous waste sites placed human health at risk. Allowing the Superfund program to live an uneventful life and die a quiet death condemned thousands of contaminated communities across the nation and caused yet unknown tolls in human suffering.

Some citizens in these contaminated communities, recognizing the classist and racial criteria of site selection, and the government's subsequent indifference, rebelled. Grassroots environmental organizations emerged that transformed members' views of the political world.

CONTAMINATED COMMUNITIES AND ENVIRONMENTAL GRIEVANCES

The new class war featured a calculated lack of regulatory enforcement that, for many citizens, contradicted the continuing revelations of contaminated communities. The environmental grievances expressed by grassroots activists in contaminated communities vary. Many communities are threatened by the toxic effects of industry, for example, and others by the toxic effects of the military. Still others raise charges of environmental racism in the distribution of industrial and military pollution.

In the following sections, we present several capsule case studies of contaminated communities in which grassroots resistance arose during the 1980s. These vignettes are taken from a report compiled by the Highlander Research and Education Center of New Market, Tennessee. The report summarizes a series of environmental workshops hosted by the Highlander Center and attended by representatives of community-based grassroots environmental groups.

Grievances in Industry-Contaminated Communities

Wyandotte County near Kansas City is a working-class community, the smallest and one of the poorest counties in the state of Kansas. Yet Wyandotte County contains sixty-nine Superfund sites. Contamination derives from several sources, most notably a chromium replating business that dumped lead, chromium, and cyanide into the sewer system; a medical waste incinerator that burns 18 tons of hazardous wastes per day; two soap companies that dump waste chemicals into the Kansas River; a General Motors plant; a furniture company; a waste disposal site; an electrical processing center; a manufacturer of petroleum products; several metal industries; and nine metal disposal sites. In 1988 EPA placed the chromium replating site on the National Priority List but did so quietly, without informing community members.

Toxic levels of lead have been found in the soil and water, and residents claim an increased incidence of lupus, thyroid problems, and certain types of cancer. The EPA has warned residents through local newspapers that high lead concentrations can cause damage to the brain, kidneys, nervous system, and red blood cells. Finally, county residents formed Concerned Citizens for Cleanup to monitor the cleanup and oversee health studies by the county Health Department. Group members are extremely distrustful of information produced by EPA and industry officials.

Calvert City, Kentucky, hosts ten chemical industries and a hazardous waste incinerator. Residents believe the greatest health threat they face is from the Liquid Waste Disposal (LWD), which receives over 70 percent of its waste from other states. The incinerators burn pesticides, herbicides, PCBs, chlorinated waste, military waste, and EPA Superfund cleanup wastes.

Environmental health hazards affect both LWD workers and community residents. LWD has no union. Employees have complained of radioactive exposure, hair loss, memory loss, and neurological damage. County residents claim to have the highest rate of cancer in Kentucky. In 1985 because of their belief that a cancer epidemic was in progress, citizens formed the Coalition for Health Concern, a group funded through member donations and yard sales. It insisted on air monitoring and a study of air, water, land, and human health. Members bitterly claim that coverups have occurred at nearly every level of government.

Private wells in *Auburn, Massachusetts,* are contaminated by toxic chemicals leaching from a truck stop. Operations at the truck stop resulted in dangerous levels of chlorobenzene and dichlorobenzene in the water supply. Tests on the underlying aquifer also revealed an 18-inch layer of oil and gas floating on top of the aquifer, enough to be deadly. The Maple Hill Neighborhood Association was formed to monitor the cleanup.

There are thousands of similar tales. Effluent from a North Carolina paper mill is carried into Tennessee by the Pigeon River and, in *Hartford, Tennessee* so many men have died of cancer that residents call the town "Widowville." They believe the paper mill to be the cause, and they have formed a citizens organization, Americans for a Clean Environment. Residents of *Sedalia, Missouri,* formed the Good Neighbors Group to combat the odors, explosions, spills, and leaks from a chemical plant in the community. A tanning company pollutes the Yellow Creek in *Middlesboro, Kentucky,* where Yellow Creek Concerned Citizens brought suit against the company and the city.

Grievances in Military-Contaminated Communities

The government's need for weapons of war requires production facilities in civilian sites employing civilian workers. As a consequence, some communities have been contaminated by the military. Historically, military sites have not been required to comply with the environmental laws that govern corporate production activities. Consequently, unregulated contamination at these sites has gone on for decades, hidden under the cloak of national security. Communities such as Oak Ridge, Tennessee, Livermore, California, and Fernald, Ohio, each have its own toxic tale.

Oak Ridge was the first facility developed for the Manhattan Project. The town of Oak Ridge was created to house the military and civilian workers who separated the uranium isotopes eventually used in "Little Boy"—the first atomic bomb used for military purposes. "Little Boy" was dropped on Hiroshima, Japan, on August 6, 1945; only then were Oak Ridge citizens informed about the product of their labors.

For many years, as Oak Ridge continued to play a critical role in national defense research and production, area residents denied the risks attending production activities at the military reservation. Denial was facilitated by lack of information (as a military site, Oak Ridge operated in utter secrecy) and by the residents' economic dependence on the facility.

The secrecy of Oak Ridge operations was fractured in 1983 when a citizens organization brought suit against the government and pressured for congressional hearings on mercury contamination by the military. The facility became the first weapons plant to come under close scrutiny for environmental practices. Union Carbide, the corporate contractor operating the Oak Ridge facility at the time, disclosed that more than 2 million pounds of mercury had been "lost to the environment" as a result of lithium recovery operations. At least half of the lost mercury was believed to have migrated off the 37,000-acre reservation site and to have entered the public domain.

The Oak Ridge reservation subsequently became the first U.S. military nuclear facility to be subject to state regulation for hazardous materials. More information regarding waste disposal practices has since become available. For example, open pit dumping of hazardous and radioactive waste was standard practice for forty years. Hazardous and radioactive wastes stored in underground tanks and buried in landfills have migrated off-site through streams and lie in the sediments of Tennessee's largest recreational lake. Radioactive contamination has entered the food chain; it has been publicly documented that radioactivity has been found in Oak Ridge area mosquitos, frogs, geese, and deer.

Since 1988 the citizens organization, the Oak Ridge Environmental Peace Alliance, has monitored cleanup activities in Oak Ridge. Members have protested nuclear weapons production, participated in public hearings, advocated public health studies, and affiliated with other grassroots groups to protest at other weapons sites.

The *Lawrence Livermore National Laboratory* was founded in Livermore, California, in 1952 to develop and test hydrogen bombs. It has since developed the MX missile and the Ground Launched Cruise missile. Livermore Laboratory is the birthplace of the Strategic Defense Initiative, or Star Wars. In many ways, Livermore is similar to the "company towns" found in Appalachia and other coal regions, in that the local economy is almost completely dependent on one facility. Livermore Laboratory employs around 8500 full-time workers.

The Livermore Laboratory generates about 4500 tons per year of toxic and radioactive waste, 90 percent of it produced by weapons and weapons-related programs. Subject to no environmental regulations, employees have for forty years devised their own waste disposal methods. As a consequence, the reservation contains two sites so severely contaminated that they are on the National Priority List for Superfund cleanup. A citizens organization, the Tri-Valley Citizens Against a Radioactive Environment, was founded in 1983. Members used the Freedom of Information Act to document numerous accidents, spills, and leaks at the Laboratory. Previously, such information had been kept secret from the very community residents most likely to be adversely affected by contaminants.

Members of the citizens organization maintain that the people who are directly affected by a facility have the basic right to participate in the decision-making process. A group representative described the organization's goal: "We seek to assist and empower citizens to find their voices and speak out on [Lawrence Livermore National Laboratory] issues, thus changing the imbalance of power that has existed historically between the super-secret weapons laboratory and the unquestioning community."

The federal government's *Feed Materials Production Center* began operations in 1952 at Fernald, Ohio, a town about 16 miles northwest of Cincinnati. The plant was built to process uranium for nuclear weapons and nuclear reactors. In 1984 citizens concerned about possible health effects formed the Fernald Residents for Environmental Safety and Health (FRESH) to evaluate the levels and types of contamination in the community.

FRESH members have forced the disclosure of numerous environmental problems attributable to the government plant. For example, significant portions of the Great Miami Aquifer, a source of drinking water for thousands, is contaminated, as are private wells. About 394,000 pounds of uranium were discharged to the air. More than 8 million cubic feet of chemicals and radioactive wastes are stored on-site. The Fernald site is on the National Priority List, and plans are currently underway for the Superfund cleanup. FRESH members vow that they and their descendants will remain vigilant for the many decades required to ensure cleanup.

Environmental Racism

The relationship between social class and exposure to environmental problems is made more complex by the effects of race. In 1987 the Commission for Racial Justice, appointed by the United Church of Christ, issued its report entitled "Toxic Wastes and Race: A National Report on the Racial and Socioeconomic Characteristics of Communities with Hazardous Wastes." According to the report, the commission's study demonstrates that "African-American communities and other communities of color bear a heavier burden than society at large in the disposal of the nation's hazardous waste. Race was the most potent variable in predicting the location of uncontrolled (abandoned) and commercial toxic waste sites in the United States" (Bullard and Wright 1992:41). The report indicates that three of the nation's largest commercial hazardous waste sites are located in black or Latino communities in Alabama, Louisiana, and California. These three sites represented 40 percent of the nation's total hazardous waste disposal capacity in 1987.

Historically, planners of waste disposal facilities, heavy metal operations, and chemical plants have tended to locate the noxious facilities in minority communities. Bullard and Wright argue that such decisions are made because industry officials attribute a Third World view of economic development to members of minority communities: "that is, any development is better than no development at all" (Bullard and Wright 1992:47).

Without knowledge of intent, however, it is often difficult to distinguish between the effects of race and class. In 1984, a study commissioned by the California Waste Management Board and prepared by Cerrell & Associates (known as the Cerrell Report) identified the demographic characteristics of the neighborhoods *most* and *least resistant* to hazardous waste facilities in their communities. The Cerrell Report, widely circulated in the toxics industries, clearly indicates that the easiest targets for new sites are the poorest, the most economically vulnerable communities. Thus, the report states, industry planners typically choose for their facilities the most economically vulnerable sites: working class and poor communities. Quite often, they are also minority communities.

Less ambiguous evidence of environmental racism can be found in a situation already confined to poor communities by the initial siting decision: the cleanup of already contaminated sites. In September 1992 a study released by the *National Law Journal* concluded that the federal government discriminates against minority communities in the cleanup of hazardous waste sites. The investigation showed that the penalties the EPA imposed on polluters were more lenient in minority areas and that the speed of cleanup of hazardous waste sites was slower, compared with waste sites in white areas. The report was especially critical of the EPA's cleanup efforts within minority communities in the South.

Also in September 1992, the EPA sponsored a two-day conference to discuss whether minority communities are disproportionately exposed to toxic wastes and industrial pollution. In attendance were grassroots groups that were fighting contamination in their own communities. They demanded fewer studies and greater EPA action. EPA officials promised to open a new office dedicated to what they referred to as "environmental equity."

Minorities have recently begun to challenge the legitimacy of the jobs versus environmental quality tradeoff. Bullard and Wright find that grassroots environmental action in black communities is most likely to take place when the organization's agenda includes safeguards against environmental blackmail, a focus on inequality and civil rights, an endorsement of direct action tactics, and the goal of political empowerment of the underdog (1992:42). Grassroots environmental groups typically emerge in black communities through established social action organizations such as churches, civic clubs, neighborhood associations, and community improvement organizations (Bullard and Wright 1992).

The nation's largest hazardous waste dump is Chemical Waste Management's landfill in *Emelle, Alabama*. Opened in 1978, the landfill represents about 25 percent of the nation's total hazardous waste landfill capacity. When plans for the landfill were drawn up, residents were initially told that the incoming industry, which would become the economic basis of the community, was a brick factory. Grassroots opposition emerged when residents learned that their economic salvation was actually a hazardous waste dump. Emelle, Alabama, is a largely black and economically impoverished community.

For fifty years the neighborhood of *West Dallas, Texas*, was contaminated by a local lead smelting facility. The smelter released more than 269 tons of lead particles per year into the air. In 1981 residents mobilized to close the plant and remove contaminated soil from the neighborhood. West Dallas is a low-income neighborhood in which 85 percent of the community population is black.

Institute, West Virginia, is the site of the Union Carbide chemical plant that was the prototype for the company's plant in Bhopal, India. A 1985 leak at the Institute plant hospitalized over 100 people and increased residents' concerns about another Bhopal incident. They formed a citizens organization, People Concerned about MIC, to monitor plant activities. The population of Institute, West Virginia, is 90 percent black.

In the *Piney Woods/Alton Park neighborhood of South Chattanooga, Tennessee*, residents no longer fish, play, or hunt along Chattanooga Creek. The creek and its surrounding area are severely contaminated by chemical factories, heavy metals industries, and a construction debris dump. Forty-two known toxic waste sites exist in the small community. Twenty homes are adjacent to "Residue Hill," where pesticides were dumped for two decades. The Piney Woods/Alton Park contaminated area is estimated to be about 100 times the size of the Love Canal site.

Residents of the community claim high rates of cancer and respiratory illnesses, miscarriages, and respiratory problems with newborns. According to a community activist, "Plants die before the summer is over and cars have to be repainted before they are paid for" (Highlander Research and Education Center 1992). In 1983, citizens founded the Chattanooga Community Organization to stop toxic chemical spills and air emissions. The population of the Piney Woods/Alton Park neighborhood is 98 percent black.

The *Carver Terrace Subdivision area of Texarkana, Texas*, has a long toxic history. Between 1910 and 1961 a creosote wood treatment facility was operated on the area's 62 acres. In 1964 the area was pronounced liveable, and the Carver Terrace housing subdivision was developed in the northern half of the site. A sand and gravel company operated in the southern half of the site until 1984. At that time, the Texas Department of Water Resources discovered that the neighborhood was contaminated with dangerous levels of various chemicals and metals, and the site was therefore placed on the National Priority List. Residents complained of numerous health effects: rashes, miscarriages, premature births, respiratory problems, nosebleeds, thyroid and kidney problems, bronchitis, and fibroid tumors. Residents attribute the deaths of twenty-six neighbors so far to the toxins in the neighborhood. In 1985 citizens formed the Carver Terrace Community Action Group and have successfully pressed for government relocation. The Carver Terrace neighborhood is composed of 100 percent black homeowners.

SUMMARY

The public's faith in the doctrine of economic growth at the expense of the environment wavered following reports from Love Canal and Three Mile Island. For many people, that faith was broken in the 1980s by revelations that their very own communities, their very own families, were endangered by contamination from corporate and military production processes. Confronting seemingly indifferent federal and state officials, many citizens replaced the void left by shattered faith with a growing sense of outrage and injustice—environmental injustice.

Although the initial impetus to the sense of environmental injustice varied—corporate-induced contamination, military-induced contamination, environmental racism—underlying the outrage of all of these working-class citizens was the shock of discovering that the model of democracy instilled in them since childhood was inconsistent with their experiences with the system. The sense of environmental injustice is a prelude to social change.

8. *Environmental Injustices*

Many residents of contaminated communities have experienced the effects of the corporate state structure in a way that has shaken their belief in the promise of the democratic system. The process they undergo is a kind of cognitive chain reaction that runs from the double betrayal they experience, through contamination, followed by governmental indifference, to a new commitment to democratic procedures. The spark that ignites this cognitive chain reaction is a sense of environmental injustice.

In this chapter, we first examine the concept of environmental injustice. Then we analyze the grassroots organizations that are formed to deal with environmental injustice, contrasting them with the national environmental organizations. Finally, we identify the stages that tend to characterize grassroots environmental conflicts and assess the accomplishments of the grassroots environmental movement.

ENVIRONMENTAL ISSUES AND
SOCIAL CLASS CONFLICT

Ordinary citizens—by which we mean typical American residents with the customary worries, needs, and everyday activities—frequently develop a more dynamic, participatory concept of democracy through their activism in grassroots environmental conflicts. Working-class people typically adhere strongly to a democratic ideology, so that when faced with a public problem such as an environmental threat to their community, they trust that the government will make things right, once their case is heard. Indeed, a basic guarantee of a democratic system is that it provide safeguards to protect the public from harm. Commonly, however, to their disillusionment, the grassroots environmentalists find that the government is not responsive to their needs. They begin to question the government's fulfillment of democratic ideology and eventually conclude that government remains unresponsive to the private citizen because it consistently favors the needs of powerful business interests in order to promote economic growth. Consequently, participation in grassroots environmental conflict convinces activists that the government is not there to serve the people, and so their environmental struggle is moved to a larger stage in which activists challenge centralized economic and political power. Democratic ideology becomes the activists' instrument of politicization and transformation from passive petitioner to active citizen. As Krauss writes of an environmental activist:

> Contacting regulatory agencies, attending local township meetings, and going to court are hardly radical forms of political struggle. Yet for [Frank] Kahler each of these steps created a contradiction between his expectations of what a democratic government should do and the actual goals and policies on behalf of economic growth that his government pursued. The responses of governmental institutions unmasked for him the ways in which the democratic government consistently favored the growth needs of chemical companies over the health and lives of community residents (1989:236–237).

Perceptions of environmental injustice arise when citizens come to believe that the state is failing to protect their lives and property from environmental pollution and that pollution costs are being unfairly imposed on them. This perception is shaped by structural forces, most notably the corporate state, and by citizens' experiences with it as they try to make the system work for them as promised in traditional cultural values and democratic ideology. The perception of environmental injustice generates a new form of social control: the community-based grassroots environmental organization. The organization acts as an informal control mechanism when the formal mechanism—environmental regulation—fails. Members of grassroots environmental groups challenge the distribution of the costs of local environmental pollution, and they demand better protection of their lives and property.

More specifically, the perception of environmental injustice among the working class is a complex product of three social forces operating in the 1980s. The first significant force involves the Love Canal and Three Mile Island disasters and how those events exposed, to a small but critical mass, the corporate state structure and the class interests it serves. Converging with those revelations was the consistent and deliberate program of environmental deregulation carried out by the Reagan administration. A third force was the trickledown of environmental grievances (Morrison 1986) manifested in continuing discoveries of contaminated communities.

Reagan's environmental deregulation policies and the increasing discoveries of toxic communities stimulated a strong grassroots response that demanded, not just the cleanup of toxic sites, but greater democratic participation in decisions about economic growth and production processes. Social class issues dominate the struggle between citizens of contaminated communities and the corporate-political elites, and highlight what Capek calls "the deep division between social groups that own and profit from the production of products containing toxic contaminants and those who typically live or work in places that are contaminated" (1991:1).

The middle-class wing of the environmental movement—that is, the national environmental organizations—has not been responsive to the local environmental problems faced by communities. The national organizations are often more interested in the preservation of pristine environments, while grassroots groups want to defend against or reverse the contamination of communities where people live and work, areas, whether clean or toxic, that the national groups frequently view as already lost to civilization.

Yet the divisions go beyond geographical focus to more fundamental, class-derived differences of self-interest. Although several national organizations share grassroots skepticism about the benefits of uncontrolled economic growth, their general perspective on growth is different from that of the grassroots groups. Their size and degree of professionalization necessitate the solicitation of large corporate contributions. Moreover, members of the national organizations are frequently committed to the concepts of ecological limits and sustainable growth. Consequently, they promote environmental and economic arguments for sustainable agriculture and energy conservation, and they seldom emphasize public health concerns, which are the primary issues for grassroots groups. They pursue issues such as environmental aesthetics, recreation, conservation, and preservation, and they are less likely to press issues concerning the links between economic growth and environmental degradation or human health effects. The report by the Highlander Research and Education Center on environmental workshops, discussed in the last chapter, summarizes participants' views of the "Group of 10" national environmental organizations:

> These groups were highly successful in getting original environmental laws passed. Now, they often seem content to continue to work only as an environmental lobby. In many cases, they too appear to have been coopted by the system. Community environmental activists are outraged when some of these organizations accept large amounts of money from the corporate polluters and industries that are destroying the environment. They are further outraged when these organizations have high-ranking officials from these same corporations and industries on their Boards of Directors. To compound the problem, many of these organizations serve as the self-appointed spokespersons for the environmental movement in the United States and often give all appearances of being the environmental voice for the citizens (1992:18).

The report shows that community activists believe that understanding their local environmental problems requires an understanding of a great deal more than environmental science or the local political structure. It also requires knowledge of the policy decisions that create the problems, of economic development issues, of women's issues, of racism, poverty, unemployment, and worker safety. And it requires a commitment to solutions that work, not just on the macroeconomic level, but on the level of individual workers and residents.

GRASSROOTS VERSUS NATIONAL ENVIRONMENTAL ORGANIZATIONS

In contrast to the national environmental organizations, the grassroots environmental organizations frequently consist of working-class participants, who are often people of color and women. Some grassroots groups are led by experienced community or political activists, but within the newer wing of the movement the leaders who have emerged are often housewives and mothers such as Lois Gibbs with no previous organizing experience. Some researchers suggest that women are active in grassroots environmental organizations because they are more likely than men to perceive an environmental threat to the community. Some attribute women's greater environmental concern to the *motherhood effect,* which refers to the idea that mothers worry about the effects of environmental problems like polluted water and air on their children's health and safety. Therefore, they become active in grassroots organizations to protect their children.

Other researchers suggest that working-class women are involved in grassroots environmental organizations because they have more flexible schedules and have closer ties with kin who can help with normal household chores. Working-class families are more likely than those of other social classes to follow traditional gender roles, with the men working outside the home for wages and the women working at home, caring for the children, the house, and the men. These women work, but they do not have to punch a time card and so their schedules tend to be more flexible. Women are more able than men to structure their time in a way that permits their involvement in organizational activities. Consequently, the grassroots wing of the contemporary environmental movement is largely working class and contains more women and more people of color than is true of the lobbying wing of the movement. Are such important differences between the two wings manifested in different organizational goals?

While national environmental organizations negotiate with congressional members over versions of environmental legislation that, from the grassroots view, differ very little one from the other, grassroots environmental groups emphasize environmental justice. *Environmental justice* refers to the belief that both environmental benefits and environmental costs should be equally distributed in society, and that corporations should be obligated to obey existing laws, just as individuals are so obligated. As a consequence, members of grassroots environmental organizations are characteristically much less willing than those of the national groups to compromise on environmental issues. Grassroots activists typically combat some immediate health threat posed by environmental pollution to their family and community members. They are not likely to bargain over degrees of illness.

The motivating factor in most grassroots conflicts is a desire to protect the health and safety of families against some perceived environmental threat. The threat may derive from a longstanding environmental problem, such as the leaking Love Canal landfill; it may involve a suddenly imposed environmental problem, such as the partial meltdown at TMI; or the threat may be generated by the anticipated toxic effects of a proposed industry, landfill, or incinerator. Industrialists have assigned to those grassroots activists the label of NIMBYs—Not In My Back Yard—a pejorative term implying that the selfish citizens' only concern is that the noxious facility not exist in their own neighborhoods. Of course, the question of whether to put the facility in the CEO's back yard never arises, for obvious reasons; we all understand that the choice is between My Back Yard and another just like it. Grassroots activists' response to the label has been to claim that they are, in fact, NIABYs—Not In Anyone's Back Yard.

Grassroots activists question political and corporate assessments of environmental risk that are based on cost-benefit analyses. Implicit in their actions is a challenge to the prevalent belief that economic growth is absolutely good and that its benefits ultimately trickle down to everyone. Community groups opposing a new noxious facility are unwilling to trade their families' welfare for some alleged benefits to the society as a whole. Thus, grassroots groups have implicitly contested the assumptions of cost-benefit analysis by identifying who pays most of the costs and who gets most of the benefits. Accepting the idea that the unequal distribution of *benefits* will continue, they dispute the contention that the distribution of *costs* should be determined by the same measure. These groups have questioned the rights of corporations to make decisions without community input, particularly when those corporate decisions have health and social consequences for other community members. This challenge to the traditional corporate right of making economic decisions without public participation is an inherently radical one, implying opposition to and a desire to change the corporate state structure itself. The challenge of the grassroots groups carries the potential for significant social change.

Through their participation in grassroots environmental conflicts, activists come to view environmental injustices as further examples of the myriad of social inequalities that the working class endures. Grassroots activism is often a radicalizing experience for group members. Over time, they frequently change their goals, from opposing an isolated environmental threat at the local level to struggling for environmental justice at the national and international levels.

In stark contrast to the professionalized leadership and staff of the national environmental groups, almost all grassroots environmental groups depend entirely on volunteers to carry out their work. Working-class people have typically been highly critical of protest activities. Yet, when confronted with an environmental threat to their community, many find themselves going beyond the more traditional tactics of petitioning government officials: initiating lawsuits to enforce environmental standards, and taking up bull horns, spray paint, and picket signs. When people feel that their families' health is at stake, they sometimes take actions that violate community standards of acceptable behavior: Notably, they engage in civil disobedience and occasionally even break the law. The environmental struggle often becomes a dominant passion in their lives, and they adopt new social roles: speaking in public, arguing with political leaders, researching and studying topics such as chemistry and environmental law, and interacting with lawyers and other experts.

Lois Gibbs, for example, the founder of LCHA at Love Canal, was a working-class housewife with no aspirations for a career or obligations beyond that provided by her family. She has described herself as shy and retiring prior to her activism. Yet, for the health of her family, she forced herself to go door-to-door, collecting support and eliciting frightening stories about illnesses. Buoyed by LCHA's success, Gibbs in 1981 founded the Citizens Clearinghouse on Hazardous Wastes (CCHW), a relatively unique mix between a national organization and a grassroots organization dedicated to grassroots environmentalism at the community level. CCHW has a paid staff, with scientific and legal consultants. Members organize national conferences for activists, offer leadership training, publish newsletters and manuals, provide technical assistance to community groups, develop policy papers and legislative initiatives, channel grassroots concerns to legislators, and lobby for legislation to strengthen the role of neighborhood organizations.

TYPICAL STAGES OF GRASSROOTS ENVIRONMENTAL CONFLICT

Not every community confronting an environmental threat engages in conflict. When the challenge to authorities does occur, it requires the transformation of people's perceptions of their world and of themselves, and this transformation typically occurs in stages. Initially, local authorities lose legitimacy in the eyes of community residents and are blamed for the adverse environmental conditions. These residents redefine laws, and sometimes institutions, as unjust and immoral. When citizens have stripped authorities of legitimacy, they are ready to develop a new sense of efficacy. This new self-confidence assures them that their efforts can affect the conditions of their lives. The shift in consciousness generates defiance, and when their defiance is merged with that of others in a sustained complaint, the collective response of grassroots mobilization occurs.

Changes in the perception of legitimacy and efficacy, and the emergence of a collective response require that people assign salience to the environmental problem in a way they did not before. The problem may have been suddenly imposed or it may have been a consistent feature of community life, but until individuals perceive it as immediate and personal—salient—the environmental problem will not generate grassroots mobilization. A sense of salience ignites protest. It focuses attention and primes a sense of outrage at inequality and injustice. When the sense of outrage goes unaddressed or is prolonged by the connivance of authorities, the people's bonds to authorities are further frayed. Unresponsive to claims for redress, local and federal authorities lose their legitimacy in the eyes of the people.

Kurt Finsterbusch, in his analysis of twenty-five case studies of community exposures to toxic wastes, found that the most common pattern of grassroots environmental conflict "was for the victims to experience a nuisance, ask the government to investigate and solve the problem, receive inadequate and often incompetent government responses, and pressure for a more adequate government action. . . . [C]itizen activism is generally a response to government inactivity or failure" (1989:65). In other words, citizens typically move from an individual to a collective sense of discontent. Then they present an appeal to government and collectively react to the perceived inadequacy of the government's response. Now let's examine the typical stages in grassroots environmental conflicts.

Emergence and Early Mobilization of Citizens

Individual dissatisfaction occurs prior to collective dissatisfaction and environmental conflict, whether the dissatisfaction derives from an environmental threat that is *suddenly imposed,* one that is *anticipated,* or a *longstanding* one. That is, individual citizens are upset, for varying lengths of time, before they decide to form an organization to wage the environmental battle. The spark that ignites the conflict may be a specific energizing event or a series of such events: a government or bureaucratic edict, an activist's speech, a sudden illness or death, or the provocation of an opponent may prod citizens to imbue an issue with the salience necessary to generate grassroots environmental conflict.

The energizing event for environmental conflict based on *suddenly imposed* environmental problems is the abrupt appearance of the problem itself. At TMI, for example, environmental conflict was ignited by the nuclear power accident and the perceived ineptitude of officials in handling it. Citizen action against Union Carbide Corporation's Institute, West Virginia, plant only emerged after a chemical leak caused evacuation, and the public perceived a salient link between this incident and the disaster at Bhopal, India.

Energizing events for environmental conflicts over *anticipated* environmental threats typically take the form of a public announcement of the intention to locate a facility such as a landfill or a waste incinerator—or, occasionally, a particularly noxious industry—in a community. The residents of Rodman, New York, for example, were moved to environmental conflict when a regional political agency announced the construction of a massive landfill in an area prized for its environmental beauty. Concerned first about conservation issues, residents came to fear the health and safety consequences of a large landfill (Cable and Degutis 1991).

In the case of a *longstanding* environmental problem, the energizing event may be an official pronouncement of a problem. For example, residents of Love Canal had been aware of a problem in their neighborhood, which they traced to the schoolyard erected on a landfill. Although they were concerned about health problems as individual families, most were not moved to collective action until the New York State health commissioner defined the situation as an emergency and a serious threat to residents' health and safety. The Love Canal Homeowners Association was quickly organized for the coming battle.

The energizing event for environmental conflict based on longstanding environmental problems may sometimes be a series of events or a convergence of facilitating factors. For example, in the Appalachian region of eastern Kentucky, a 14-mile stretch of water known as Yellow Creek had been polluted by chemical wastes from a tanning company for nearly 100 years. For decades, individuals had registered complaints with various city and state officials, but to no avail. Despite numerous fish kills, a nauseating stench, and visible pollution in the form of three-foot waves of black foam cresting the water, residents did not collectively resist and wage environmental conflict until 1980 when they formed a grassroots environmental organization, Yellow Creek Concerned Citizens. The reasons why conflict emerged at that time and not before are complex.

First, the effects of economic repression inhibited collective efforts prior to 1980. A social legacy of the coal companies' earlier economic oppression of the area was cultural balkanization. The small isolated communities that dot the valley today are the remnants of the old coal camps, the self-contained communities built by coal companies to house miners. To hinder union organizing in the coal fields during the 1930s, coal company officials induced competition among the camps by encouraging baseball clubs and other competitive sports events. This competitiveness extended into social relations in general, so that hostility and mistrust characterized relationships among residents of the various coal camps. When the coal companies left, hostilities and intercommunity suspicions remained. These interaction patterns persisted until the 1970s, when the system of small rural schools was replaced with a consolidated school system that cut across community boundaries. The younger generation identified much less strongly with their communities of birth than did their parents. As friendships among teenagers spanned communities, parents were dragged along and community boundaries soon weakened. People began to talk to one another, and they discovered far more similarities, including grievances, than differences.

A second factor in this convergence that produced environmental conflict in the Yellow Creek Valley was the prominence of the national environmental movement in the 1970s. The national movement built an ideological foundation that legitimated a definition of environmental injustice and led to the passage of national environmental legislation that gave citizens a legal foundation for environmental conflict. A final significant factor was the return to the valley of a native, Larry Wilson, who possessed the political and organizational skills to establish and effectively structure the grassroots organization.

Energizing events help focus and concentrate individual dissatisfactions. This crystallization then engenders the formation of a grassroots environmental organization as the base from which to carry out environmental conflict. Mobilization generally takes place through previously established social networks and/or through public meetings in which concerned residents are able to identify one another. These established social networks may be occupational, friendship, or neighborhood networks; that is, typically, concerned residents talk about their environmental concerns first with those with whom they interact on an everyday basis—coworkers, friends, relatives, or neighbors. Those who become active in the grassroots organization urge their acquaintances to join also.

In contrast, interpersonal social networks were not used for mobilization at TMI. Many residents in the area immediately adjacent to the nuclear power plant were either employed by the utility company or derived their livelihoods from companies dependent on the utility company's presence. Therefore, when environmental conflict emerged between concerned citizens and the utility company, citizens hesitated to urge friends and acquaintances who were economically tied to the plant to actively oppose it. As a consequence, the grassroots organizations at TMI mobilized most effectively through public meetings and hearings. The meetings were arranged by political and utility officials, supposedly as a forum for presenting residents with accurate information about the effects of the accident. Instead, the meetings served as a way for concerned residents to identify one another, forming a basis for mobilization.

At both Love Canal and Yellow Creek, public meetings served as supplementary, rather than primary, routes of mobilization. LCHA was initially mobilized by Lois Gibbs's recruiting members door-to-door, primarily women, but the subsequent public meetings on the health threat brought in more people. At Yellow Creek, the city council meetings fulfilled this mobilization role. Verbal confrontations between elected officials and angry residents first drew large audiences because of the circuslike atmosphere. Attendance was so high for one period of time that a number of meetings had to be held in the Armory to accommodate the large crowds. Many of those who came as spectators and were not personally threatened by the stream's pollution quickly became sympathizers and members, especially when they witnessed politicians' cavalier attitudes toward residents' environmental concerns.

Once organized, grassroots environmental groups typically begin by attempting to document a hazard and link it to a current or potential health problem, such as a cluster of cancer cases or a series of adverse reproductive outcomes. This activity often leads to extensive interactions with scientists, public health officials, and sometimes lawyers.

Appeal to Authorities

When group members believe that an association exists between an actual or potential exposure and human health, they attempt to persuade government or the industry to clean up, shut down, or abandon plans to build the facility. The group's initial objective is to correct a specific problem, not to effect broader policy changes. Failure to achieve goals at this level can lead groups to enter the legal system by filing lawsuits or to move into the political arena where they endorse candidates favorable to their viewpoint or propose ballot initiatives.

Ideally, environmental regulation should involve the federal government's intervention in the economy to protect the public from exposure to environmental hazards. Because of the inherent tension in liberal democratic states, however, the government's emphasis on capital accumulation to foster economic growth has made it a largely ineffective agent of social control over environmental problems caused by corporations. Often, government actions actually encourage the corporate externalization of environmental costs. As a result of the state's contradictory roles, "regulation is an outcome of social conflict. . . . It is the politically constructed 'resolution' of social struggle" (Shover, Clelland, and Lynxwiler 1986:9). At times, grassroots environmental organizations may use the state as a tool to obtain environmental reform, generating social conflict by demanding observance of the state's legitimacy function.

Litigation

When citizens perceive that the regulatory system has failed to protect them, they frequently turn to the courts inasmuch as few alternatives exist for them. A corporation is a legal entity, and litigation is the only way to attack it. In grassroots environmental conflicts, citizen litigants typically press the government to enforce existing environmental legislation, to force corporations and government agencies to obey laws as they feel obligated to do, and they seldom propose new, more restrictive laws. However, entering a litigation phase can be harmful to the grassroots organization, for some loss of support is typical, as attention and resources increasingly turn to litigation and the requisite experts.

The change to a litigation strategy changes the nature of the grassroots organization's activities from recruitment and confrontation to grant writing and attendance at hearings. Grant writing becomes an organizational task in a litigation phase because litigation requires large amounts of money for lawyers, expert witnesses and their laboratory costs, and various court costs. A working-class community is squeezed dry fairly quickly, and other sources of funds become necessary, or the polluter will win simply by virtue of having the resources to endure. Acquiring information on foundations and grant writing usually take place through social networks with other, sometimes national, environmental organizations such as the Citizens Clearinghouse on Hazardous Wastes and the National Toxics Campaign.

A litigation strategy also produces a significant change in the division of labor within the grassroots organization caused by required attendance at various types of hearings. Litigation spawns numerous hearings and meetings that are typically held on weekdays, and may be located nearby, at the state capital, or at EPA's regional headquarters. The last two locations frequently require significant traveling time, and as a result, members usually lose a day's pay and inflict wear and tear on their cars. The necessary expenses to sustain such efforts can strain organizational and individual budgets. Often the easiest recourse is for women homemakers to bear the weight of these responsibilities. Working-class women, who, as noted earlier, customarily adhere to traditional gender roles and therefore are available during the day to attend hearings and have more flexible time schedules than men, are pressed by necessity to adopt new organizational roles and represent the group at meetings. As discussed earlier, this necessity is another reason why women are so visible in grassroots environmental conflicts.

Transformation and Evolution / Dissolution

An unanticipated, and often lasting, effect of members' activities in grassroots environmental conflicts is frequently a dramatic change in political consciousness. The experience diminishes their faith in government and business, and their willingness to move beyond mainstream activities may lead to changes in the local political structure. Grassroots environmentalists begin to see that the patterns revealed in environmental conflict reflect broader inequities of economic and political power in society, with the result that the concept of environmental justice emerges and guides them to raise questions, not only about public health, but also about political power in general.

Grassroots environmental organizations can enhance community solidarity to the extent that residents undergo a collective change of consciousness. The shift in consciousness may be manifested in efforts to change the local political structure in order to reduce the inequity in the balance of power between elites and nonelites. This collective change of consciousness is similar to the individual process of conversion and is referred to as the transformation of community consciousness (Cable and Degutis 1991). Such a transformation can occur even if the specific goals of the grassroots organization are not achieved. In fact, it might be more likely to occur if organization goals are not met, since activists may attribute the failure to "the system," and there also place the cure.

ACCOMPLISHMENTS BY THE GRASSROOTS

Environmental sociologists Riley Dunlap and Angela Mertig suggest that "history will surely record the environmental movement as among the few that significantly changed our society" (1992:xi). How has society been changed? Freudenberg and Steinsapir addressed this question by separating the achievements of the grassroots environmental movement as a whole from those of the national environmental organizations (1992:31–35). By their estimation, grassroots organizations have had at least six beneficial consequences for the public.

First, grassroots efforts have increased control over a number of environmentally noxious facilities by cleaning up contaminated sites, blocking construction of new facilities, and upgrading corporate pollution control equipment. These victories combined to produce an even greater victory, one that was both the initial motivation and the ultimate goal of these groups: improvements in public health.

Second, grassroots organizations have forced some corporations to consider the environmental costs of their production processes. In many cases, the negative publicity generated by the organizations made continued production unprofitable or led to the installation of improved pollution control devices.

Third, grassroots groups together created significant political and economic pressures on corporations and government to seek preventive approaches to environmental contamination. For example, in California certain toxic substances were banned from being discharged into drinking water, and in Massachusetts, corporations were ordered to reduce their use of toxic chemicals in production processes. Clearly, eliminating toxic chemicals from the production process is much more effective in avoiding pollution than is the use of post-production, pollution control devices.

Fourth, grassroots organizations have operated as self-help groups in communities affected by toxic disasters, functioning as social support networks that help victims understand and channel their grief and anger. By offering a vehicle to make the experience of the disaster meaningful, grassroots organizations help mitigate some of the damaging psychological consequences of toxic chemical disasters.

Fifth, the grassroots environmental movement has influenced public attitudes toward the environment and public health. A national poll in 1989 showed that 80 percent of the population agreed with the following statement (although we suspect that a more discriminating instrument would reveal some variation within that group): "Protecting the environment is so important that requirements and standards cannot be too high, and continuing environmental improvements must be made regardless of the cost" (*New York Times* poll, June 1989).

Sixth, grassroots organizations have contributed to an expansion of citizens' rights to participate in environmental decision making and, by extension, other areas of decision making. Right-to-know laws are now on the books, which, in theory at least, enable citizens to learn the names and quantities of hazardous chemicals that local factories store or emit into the water and air. Another example of expanded citizens' rights is a federal grants program that offers up to $50,000 to local groups at EPA-identified contaminated sites to hire their own technical advisers.

These changes are significant. Indeed, if, as we have stated, public sanitation represents the single greatest improvement hitherto in public health, then logic would dictate that public desanitation—the chemical rather than bacteriological defilement of the communal environment—must represent the greatest threat to public health.

The grassroots environmental movement has improved the lives of many citizens and spread environmental awareness among the public. But what of democracy and the political disillusionment of grassroots activists?

9. In Search of Environmental Justice

The word *democracy* is derived from the Greek *demokratia,* which means "rule of the people." In this purist form, democracy has never existed; it is what founding sociologist Max Weber called an *ideal type,* which refers to a concept constructed to portray the essential properties of a phenomenon. The term *ideal* has nothing to do with moral evaluation; it merely refers to an abstraction, or tool, whose use makes generalizations simpler because supposedly minor differences can be ignored in order to emphasize major similarities. Thus, an ideal type is a clean model, free of distractions, against which actual cases can be compared.

When an actual case of grassroots environmental conflict is compared to the democratic ideal, the discrepancy is huge. Even if we use the ideal type of our particular system—a representative democracy in which officials are held accountable to citizens through periodic elections—grassroots environmental conflicts reveal that the majority does not rule. Instead, power and privilege are concentrated in a few hands, and political institutions work most fundamentally in the interests of those few political and economic elites. The choice made by the citizenry, a choice initially circumscribed by elites in the early parts of the selection process, is that of which elite will hold office, and even the officeholder faces an accountability that is largely symbolic. As sociologist Robert S. Lynd described it, the problem of democracy "concerns principally the fact that purportedly democratic political institutions operate upon a factually undemocratic class base appropriate to capitalism" (1957:41).

Issues are decided by power, and solutions reached in negotiations between powerholders will reflect the balance of power between them. In any examination of grassroots environmental conflicts—what Heskin (1991) eloquently refers to as "the struggle for community"—power differentials between the adversaries are immediately apparent. Power may derive from a number of sources, and the grassroots organizations seek to balance with numbers what they lack elsewhere. The essential question inherent in grassroots environmental conflict, and a question which you as

116

a citizen of the world must eventually resolve for yourself, is this: Who should make the decisions that may result in dangerous environmental consequences? Corporate and governmental officials? The public at large? The citizens whose environment, and personal health, will be directly affected?

In this final chapter, we first examine the grassroots movement's efforts to make our political and economic institutions more democratic. We conclude with some speculations on the potential of the grassroots segment for carrying out social class conflict.

Grassroots environmental organizations have emerged since 1978, but grassroots organizations that formed around other issues have a longer tradition. In some ways, the newer organizations represent a resumption of a thread of public life that was interrupted in the 1930s. During the years from the beginning of the Industrial Revolution to the start of the New Deal, civil unrest, grassroots and organized protest, and outright class war that frequently ended in appalling violence were prominent features of American public life. This phase came to an end with the egalitarian efforts of the New Deal, followed quickly and dramatically by the collaborative crusade against the extremes of injustice, as most Americans regarded World War II, which gave lower and middle-class citizens confidence that the power of the U.S. government, the Constitution, and moral superiority would stand together with them against all dangers and oppressors, foreign and domestic.

This confidence lasted until the 1960s, when the Vietnam War and the deep divisions it produced in American society shook it profoundly. Since the 1960s, after a century-long trend in which the locus of political participation shifted from the community to the central government, an emerging feature of the American political landscape has been the proliferation of a variety of community-based grassroots organizations designed to bring about a more just and democratic political system for their constituencies through their influence on local political conditions and structures (Evans and Boyte 1986; Greider 1992). Together, these grassroots organizations may be viewed as part of a broader social movement whose general goal is "redemocratizing the United States' political system" (Rader 1992:1).

More and more often, these grassroots organizations begin with a focus on an environmental threat to the community: toxic contamination from local industrial production processes or waste disposal facilities. The increase of community exposure to environmental toxic hazards has been called "the plague of our time" (Edelstein 1988:1) and "a new species of trouble" (Erikson 1991:11). Brown exposes the slow poisoning of Americans by toxic wastes (1979) and tracks a "toxic cloud" of air pollutants across the country (1987). Using a database compiled from government and nonprofit organizational sources on environmental and public health statistics, Goldman cites the following: "Across the United States, an average of four industrial accidents a day spill toxic chemicals into the environment. Factory mishaps release 370 thousand tons of toxins into the air each year. Industrial plants routinely discharge another 7 million tons of toxic chemicals into the air and water, and dump another 500 million tons of hazardous wastes into the ground" (1991:4).

In examining grassroots activities directed against economic growth, Krauss argues that the federal government legitimized its expanded participation in the private economy by promising that it would absorb the economic and social costs of economic growth—unemployment, inflation, environmental pollution, and neighborhood deterioration: "In so doing, the state assumed an unprecedented role on behalf of working people, creating popular expectations that the state would protect them from the abuses of the private economy. In other words, the state compensated for its increased participation in the private economy by expanding democratic expectations" (1989:230).

The public's faith in the doctrine of economic growth at the expense of the environment was shaken by the incidents at Love Canal and TMI and was further eroded by trends in the 1980s: the Reagan administration's antagonism toward environment regulation and the rapidly lengthening list of communities found to be contaminated. The national environmental organizations were of little help to their grassroots counterparts, who perceived them as part of the very structure that was oppressing them. What recourse was left for residents of contaminated communities? Grassroots environmental organizations.

This is not to say that the national environmental groups have made no lasting achievements that have benefited working-class America, nor do we imply that this is the only significant criterion for judging their achievements. The efforts of national organizations have been critical in gaining significant improvements in environmental protection, particularly in the areas of air and water quality. Moreover, legislation for which the national organizations have successfully lobbied very often forms the legal basis for the litigation brought by grassroots organizations. On the other hand, the failures of the national organizations are notable: "Toxic waste problems remain largely out of control" (Buttel 1990:359). The result has been grassroots environmental conflict pitting community-based grassroots organizations against corporate and government entities. These conflicts "generally tend to be resolved either by a show of force or through legal processes, so that we find ourselves in an era of demonstrations and noisy campaigns as well as prolonged battles in the courts and legislatures" (Beneviste 1981:3).

The rapid emergence of grassroots environmental organizations in the past fifteen years has changed the contours of the contemporary environmental movement, splitting the movement in two and revealing that environmental issues are yet one more stage on which social class conflicts are played out. Viewing environmental conflicts as social class conflicts reveals the real cause underlying charges of environmental elitism within the environmental movement. Compared to the grassroots wing of the contemporary environmental movement, the national organizations are clearly composed of elites. These two wings of the environmental movement, for the most part, serve the interests of different social classes.

Let's take one more look at the significant characteristics of these two groups: One wing consists of the older, national organizations such as the Sierra Club, the National Wildlife Federation, Friends of the Earth, the Environmental Defense Fund, the Natural Resources Defense Council, and the Wilderness Society. The leaders and members of these organizations tend to be upper or upper middle-class and white. Upper and upper middle-class children are socialized to see the political economic system as theirs to manipulate, influence, and direct. Therefore, for them political activism, including environmental activism, is an extension of other political activities such as voting and staying informed. They generally have secure and meaningful jobs (or even real money) and comfortable positions in the social order, that is, they have a stake in the status quo. Their grievances, though often deeply held, concern the quality of their lives and the kind of world in which they want to live. Rather than challenging the system itself, they seek new environmental laws and improved enforcement. Consequently, environmental activism does not change their view of the political structure, and they are not radicalized by their experiences.

The second and newer wing of the contemporary environmental movement is made up of local grassroots organizations that emerge in response to environmental threats within their own communities. According to the Citizens Clearinghouse on Hazardous Wastes, some 7000 such grassroots environmental organizations have formed since the Love Canal and Three Mile Island disasters. These grassroots environmental organizations typically consist of ordinary citizens, working-class activists whose experiences with the corporate state structure induced a sense of environmental injustice.

In contrast with their upper class counterparts, working-class children are socialized to be dutiful citizens, and are taught that political democracy and corporate capitalism go hand in hand. In return for obeying the rules that others make, the working class also expects the rules to protect them. Their relationship with the corporate state structure, though still based on self-interest, is not one of manipulation but one of trust. Their grievances tend to revolve around the conditions in their immediate environment that threaten their health or their very lives and those of their children. They have no stake in the status quo that compares with the enormity of their grievances, and not even their most basic cultural beliefs remain sacrosanct if they come into conflict with their own or their children's survival.

Most residents of contaminated communities, like most residents of most communities everywhere, at first assume that the political and regulatory processes are fair. They also hold a faith in scientific experts. Those assumptions of fairness and objectivity are shattered when, in confronting the environmental threat to their community, members of grassroots organizations come to believe that they disproportionately bear the environmental costs of industrial production. Residents of contaminated communities experience a jolting inversion of democratic ideology. The intensity and power of the cause of environmental justice wells from this deep sense of betrayal. Activists challenge the distribution of environmental burdens based on race, class, gender, and power, and, quite often, the bitterness of the outrage eventually gives way to a determination to avoid further injustices. In his description of community mobilization following the nuclear accident at TMI, Walsh writes: "The conflict between local residents and authorities evolved into a political confrontation with implications for the relationship between economic growth and democracy" (1988:1). This statement is a succinct summary of all grassroots environmental conflicts.

The working-class residents of contaminated communities face serious obstacles in gaining a voice in decisions that affect them, even after they have organized a grassroots environmental group, because they typically lack the political, legal, and scientific resources that their opponents have. Residents petition elites for help and discover their own disenfranchisement. When they recognize that the existing distribution of power provided the initial conditions necessary for the contamination of their community, they begin to emphasize social class issues. Activists then perceive that the wrongs done them in the environmental sphere are part of an historical pattern of wrongs, a pattern that relates to social class. Through their environmental activism they begin to discover the true political and economic processes that are usually hidden from them behind the cultural value of democracy, and they become disenchanted with the power structure.

An explicit class rhetoric surfaces among group members, and the new class-based interpretations that they make contribute to their empowerment. When activists take this broader view, they expand their goals from the initial one of cleaning up the local community to the much larger, more inclusive goal of environmental justice. From there they may undergo another evolution in which they seek greater social justice and equality of all kinds. Thus, environmental activism is a strongly politicizing experience, and the grassroots organization becomes a vehicle for self-empowerment. The "dawning consciousness of class injustice" (Capek 1991:23) is a powerful motivator for social change.

Several analysts who have identified this burgeoning cluster of democratically oriented grassroots organizations as the new American populism refer to "the actions of groups of people seeking to gain a measure of control from forces dominating their lives" (Heskin 1991:1). Populist actions empower citizens to challenge established political structures and procedures. Through empowerment, citizens transform their relationships with powerful social groups, developing democratic consciousness and skills and increasing their control over their everyday lives. Empowerment requires the building of a political culture in which democratic politics can occur (Fisher 1993); movements of empowerment expand, even redefine, democracy. Populist movements represent a new form of politics, what Boyte has termed "a citizen-based politics" that "requires neither cynical manipulation nor civic virtue. It grows out of grassroots networks that have discovered that working around local issues, while stressing the revitalization of public life, is a powerful way of sustaining commitments" (1990:513).

In a comparison of two grassroots environmental organizations, Cable and Degutis find that the transformation of individuals was reflected in changes in the local political structure. They write that grassroots environmental conflicts "can enhance solidarity to the extent that residents undergo a collective change of consciousness which is manifested in a particular behavior: efforts to change the local political structure in such a way that there is less inequity in the balance of power between elites and non-elites" (1991:391). Viewed in this way, working-class grassroots environmental organizations constitute a social force with the potential to alter significantly the structures of our basic social institutions. For the greater the public participation in decisions that have environmental consequences, the closer we move to the ideal of democracy but the further we move from the dictates of private ownership. And private ownership is the foundation of the capitalist economic institution. The alternative to accommodating working-class demands for greater participation in the environmental decisions that affect them is greater repression. Which way will we go?

In a number of countries, including some in Latin America and Eastern Europe, public outrage over pollution-related illness and death has developed into civil unrest and open rebellion, and even contributed strongly to revolution. When their lives and those of their families are at stake, the citizens' repertoire of viable options becomes nearly boundless; it is a conflict they cannot permit themselves to lose.

Could the United States reach the point of insurrection? Of course, it could. Yet our system, flawed as it is, does possess the flexibility and responsiveness to address a grievance of such enormity and gravity. But people may rebel at death and only complain about disease. And our history, reflecting both the strengths and weaknesses of democracy, has been one of mollification rather than resolution. Will this be enough?

We unavoidably face a fundamental dilemma. Economic growth affords a high standard of living, but it also contributes to the disruptions of the biosphere that threaten both biological survival and future economic growth itself. We have two alternatives. First, we can pay now by internalizing the social costs of production and compelling regulatory compliance, which will allow environmentally responsible corporations the economic freedom from the cost-reduction pressures applied by less concerned competitors to protect the environment. The tradeoff is difficult. If we want environmental safety and preservation, we may have to live with diminished expectations about consumption and material life, which means a lower standard of living. Or, second, we can pay later, with increased environmental risks to our lives; with the loss of future economic growth when resources are depleted; and, some deeply believe, with the lives and livelihoods of our children and grandchildren.

Glossary

Accumulation   One of the fundamental functions of the liberal democratic state. Accumulation refers to the state's obligation to create and maintain the conditions under which profitable capital accumulation is possible. The other fundamental function of the state is legitimization, which sometimes comes into conflict with the function of accumulation.

Adjudicatory hearings   Adjudicatory hearings are formal legal proceedings in which involved parties may present oral testimony, cross-examine opposing witnesses, and have their cases directed by attorneys.

Anthropocentrism   The view of the environment in which people are seen as the central focus—the most important species—of the natural world. All other forms of life exist solely for the benefit of people.

Atmosphere   The air we breathe. The atmosphere is gaseous, and it extends above the earth's surface. The atmosphere, lithosphere, hydrosphere, and biosphere make up the earth's life support system.

Basic Principles of Ecosystem Function   (1) Resources are supplied and wastes are disposed of by recycling all elements. (2) Ecosystems run on solar energy, which is exceedingly abundant, nonpolluting, and relatively constant and everlasting. (3) Large biomasses cannot be supported at the ends of long food chains.

Bioaccumulation   The biological process in which small, seemingly harmless doses received over a long period of time accumulate in the body until they reach toxic levels and cause harm. Bioaccumulation occurs because the chemicals are nonbiodegradable and because they are excreted from the body only very slowly, if at all. Bioaccumulation is compounded in the food chain.

Biomagnification   The compounded effects of bioaccumulation in the food chain. Substances absorbed by organisms accumulate in their tissues. As each organism higher up on the food chain feeds, it accumulates still higher concentrations in its tissues. And so on up the food chain.

Biosphere   Those parts of the lithosphere, atmosphere, and hydrosphere in which living organisms are found. The biosphere contains all plant and animal resources and all the water, minerals, oxygen, nitrogen, phosphorus, and other nutrients that living things need. The biosphere, lithosphere, atmosphere, and hydrosphere make up the earth's life support system.

Butterfly Effect A belief half-jokingly held among weather forecasters to account for the inaccuracy of weather forecasts as they are projected further into the future. It is the notion that a butterfly taking off today in Beijing can affect next month's weather in New York. The more accurate term is *sensitive dependence on initial conditions*. Applicable to many systems, it means that tiny differences in input can quickly become overwhelming differences in output.

Carrying capacity The maximum population of a given animal—including people—that an ecosystem can support without being degraded or destroyed in the long run. The carrying capacity can be exceeded but not without lessening the system's ability to support life in the long run.

Co-carcinogens Substances that do not, by themselves, cause cancer but that can cause cancer in combination with some other substance.

Consumers Organisms that feed directly or indirectly on producers; one of the four components of the ecosystem. Consumers are animals, including herbivores, carnivores, and omnivores—and people. The other components of the ecosystem are producers, detritus feeders, and decomposers.

Corporate capitalism Modern form of capitalism characterized by a concentration of wealth.

Decomposers Organisms whose feeding activity decays dead plant and animal matter; one of the four components of the ecosystem. The other components are producers, consumers, and detritus feeders.

Detritus feeders Organisms that consume dead plant and animal matter directly; one of the four components of the ecosystem. Some examples of detritus feeders are vultures, earthworms, and termites. The other components of the ecosystem are producers, consumers, and decomposers.

Economic growth An increase in the capacity of the economy to provide goods and services for final use.

Ecosystem All the populations of plant and animal species that live and interact in a given area at a particular time, as well as the chemical and physical factors that make up the nonliving environment. An ecosystem may be an ocean, a tropical rainforest, a fallen log, or a puddle of water. All of the earth's ecosystems put together make up the biosphere.

Environmental degradation Disruptions to the environment that have negative consequences for ecosystems. Environmental degradation involves both *withdrawals* to the environment and *additions* to it.

Environmental justice The belief that both environmental benefits and environmental costs should be equally distributed in society and that corporations should be obligated to obey existing laws the same as individuals are so obligated.

Environmental regulation Government intervention in the economy to establish standards for production processes by corporations. Rather than permitting prices and market forces to affect economic behavior freely, the government intervenes to specify through laws what may and may not be done.

Environmental sociology The scientific study of people's beliefs about the environment, their behavior toward it, and the ways in which the structure of society influences them and contributes to the persistent abuse of the environment.

Externalization of the environmental costs of production Externalizing the environmental costs of production from the corporation to the public. In an economic system that relies on continuous economic growth, corporations are able to avoid paying for the damages that production processes inflict on the environment. Any environmental problems then become public rather than corporate problems.

Force The use of power whose basis is the threat or application of punishment.

Government The individuals and groups who control the state apparatus and direct state power. This is in contrast to the state, which is a social organization.

Growth coalition The alliance among corporations, the state, and the working class in support of economic growth.

Hazardous waste Any discarded materials that could pose a serious threat to human health or to the environment.

Heavy metals Metallic elements that in pure form are heavy; that is, they have high atomic weights. Some examples are lead, mercury, arsenic, cadmium, tin, chromium, zinc, and copper. Heavy metals are extremely toxic because, being soluble in water, they can be ingested and absorbed by organisms.

Hydrosphere All of the earth's moisture—all of our water resources—in the forms of liquid, ice, and water vapor. The hydrosphere, lithosphere, atmosphere, and biosphere make up the earth's life support system.

Ideal type A term coined by founding sociologist Max Weber referring to a concept constructed to portray the essential properties of a phenomenon. The term *ideal* has nothing to do with moral evaluation; it merely refers to an abstraction or tool.

Interest group A voluntary organization composed of people who share a similar attitude or interest. Interest groups make special claims on other social groups and serve as intermediaries between individuals and government.

Legitimization The second fundamental function of the liberal democratic state. This function dictates that the state must create and maintain conditions of social harmony. The other fundamental function of the state is the accumulation function. These functions sometimes conflict, creating a serious dilemma for the state.

Lithosphere The solid, upper surface or crust of the earth that contains soil, land, minerals, and energy resources. The lithosphere, atmosphere, hydrosphere, and biosphere make up the earth's life support system.

Midnight dumping A practice in which entrepreneurs, for a fee, dispose of a company's hazardous wastes by dumping them illegally and then pocketing the money, leaving the toxic chemicals in any untended locations they can find.

Natural resources Things produced naturally in the physical environment that are used to meet human needs. Resources include soil, water, land, animals, plants, minerals, and energy. Natural resources are classified as perpetual resources, renewable resources, or nonrenewable resources.

Nonrenewable resources Natural resources that exist in a fixed amount in the earth's crust. They are either not replenished by natural processes, as is the case with copper, or they are replenished much more slowly than they are used, such as oil. Wilderness and rangeland resources, minerals, and fossil fuels are nonrenewable. A nonrenewable resource is considered depleted when 80 percent of its total estimated supply has been removed and used.

Perpetual resources Natural resources that come from what is essentially an inexhaustible source. Perpetual resources remain available in a relatively constant supply regardless of whether or how we use them. Examples are solar energy, winds, tides, and flowing water.

Phases of the production process Mining, transportation, manufacturing, and waste disposal. Each phase has three major effects on the environment. Each phase uses energy, depletes natural resources, and pollutes the earth.

Power The ability of individuals and groups to realize their will in human affairs, even if it involves the resistance of others.

Producers Plants, such as trees, that manufacture their own food through photosynthetic processes; one of the four components of the ecosystem. The other components are consumers, detritus feeders, and decomposers.

Professionalism An organization style characterized by the same features identified in many formal organizations: a paid, professional staff and clearly defined roles for members who fill particular positions in the organization. Professionalism characterizes the national environmental organizations, particularly in the number of lobbyists, lawyers, and scientists employed full time.

Renewable resources Natural resources that can be depleted in the short run if they are used or contaminated too rapidly but that normally can be replaced in the long run through natural processes. Renewable resources include fertile soil, forests, animal and plant resources, and surface water and groundwater.

Social institutions Formalized systems of beliefs and behavior composed of interrelated cultural norms that provide established answers and standardized solutions for basic social tasks. Some examples of social institutions are the family, religion, politics, the economy, and education.

Social stratification The structured ranking of individuals and groups into horizontal layers according to important social markers—for example, their possession of material objects or social attributes that are scarce in society and therefore highly prized.

Sociology A social science. It is the scientific study of human behavior in society, particularly the study of individuals in groups and organizations.

Solid waste Any and all unwanted and discarded materials that are not liquids or gases.

State A social organization that exercises within a given territory an effective monopoly in the use of physical coercion. This is in contrast to the government, which refers to individuals and groups.

Synergistic effects The product of the interaction of two or more substances or factors that cause a net effect greater than that expected from adding together their independent effects. That is, the total effect of the interaction of the substances is greater than the sum of two effects taken independently.

Synthetic organic chemicals Human-made, carbon-based compounds that are the basis for all plastics, synthetic fibers, solvents, pesticides, and wood preservatives. Examples are dioxins, many of which are believed to be associated with liver cancer, birth defects, headaches, weight loss, hair loss, insomnia, and nerve damage; and polychlorinated biphenyls (PCBs), used in electrical transformers and associated with liver and kidney damage, gastric disorders, reproductive disorders, skin lesions, and tumors.

Toxic chemical waste   A particular kind of hazardous waste that is widely produced in industry.

Toxic industrial wastes   Toxic chemicals generated in production processes and discarded as waste. Toxic industrial wastes must be returned or added to the biosphere.

Selected Readings

Arms, Karen. 1990. *Environmental Science.* Philadelphia: Saunders College Publishing. Chapter 3.

Barbour, Ian G. 1980. *Technology, Environment, and Human Values.* New York: Praeger. Chapters 2, 3, 4.

Bartell, Ted. 1976. "Political Orientations and Public Response to the Energy Crisis." *Social Science Quarterly* 57(September):430–436. Chapter 6.

Benveniste, Guy. 1981. *Regulation and Planning: The Case of Environmental Politics.* San Francisco: Boyd & Fraser Publishing Co. Chapters 3, 4.

Block, Fred. 1977. "The Ruling Class Does Not Rule: Notes on the Marxist Theory of the State." *Socialist Review* 7(May–June):6–28. Chapter 4.

Boggs, Carl. 1986. *Social Movements and Political Power: Emerging Forms of Radicalism in the West.* Philadelphia: Temple University Press. Chapter 8.

Bouchier, David. 1987. *Radical Citizenship: The New American Activism.* New York: Schocken Books. Chapters 8, 9.

Boyte, Harry C. 1990. "The Growth of Citizen Politics: Stages in Local Community Organizing." *DISSENT,* Fall. Chapter 9.

———. 1986. "Beyond Politics as Usual." In Harry Boyte and Frank Reissman, eds. *The New Populism: The Politics of Empowerment.* Philadelphia: Temple University Press. Chapter 9.

———. 1984. *Community Is Possible.* New York: Harper & Row. Chapter 9.

———. 1980. *The Backyard Revolution.* Philadelphia: Temple University Press. Chapter 9.

Boyte, Harry, Heather Booth, and Steve Max. 1986. *Citizen Action and the New American Populism.* Philadelphia: Temple University Press. Chapters 8, 9.

Brannigan, Augustine, and Sheldon Goldenbert, eds. 1985. *Social Responses to Technological Change.* Westport, Conn.: Greenwood Press. Chapter 4.

Brown, Michael H. 1987. *The Toxic Cloud: The Poisoning of America's Air.* New York: Harper & Row. Chapter 8.

Brown, Michael H. 1979. *Laying Waste: The Poisoning of America by Toxic Chemicals.* New York: Pantheon. Chapter 8.

Brown, Phil, and Edwin J. Mikkelsen. 1990. *No Safe Place: Toxic Waste, Leukemia, and Community Action.* Berkeley: University of California Press. Chapters 7, 8.

Note: Entries conclude with references to chapters in this book which cite them.

Buck, Susan J. 1991. *Understanding Environmental Administration and Law.* Washington, D.C.: Island Press.

Bullard, Robert D., and Beverly H. Wright. 1992. "The Quest for Environmental Equity: Mobilizing the African-American Community for Social Change." Pp. 39–50 in Riley E. Dunlap and Angela G. Mertig, eds. *American Environmentalism: The U.S. Environmental Movement, 1970–1990.* Philadelphia: Taylor & Francis. Chapter 8.

Buttel, Frederick H. 1990. "Environmental Quality and the State: Some Political-Sociological Observations on Environmental Regulation." Pp. 357–358 in Richard G. Braungart and Margaret M. Braungart, eds. *The Political Sociology of the State.* Greenwich, Conn.: JAI Press, Inc. Chapter 4.

Cable, Sherry, and Beth Degutis. 1991. "The Transformation of Community Consciousness: The Effects of Citizens' Organizations on Host Communities." *International Journal of Mass Emergencies and Disasters* 9:383–399. Chapter 8.

Cable, Sherry, and Edward J. Walsh. 1991. "The Emergence of Environmental Protest: Yellow Creek and TMI Compared." In S. R. Couch and J. S. Kroll-Smith, eds. *Communities at Risk: Collective Responses to Technological Hazards.* New York: Peter Lang Publishing. Chapter 8.

Cable, Sherry, Edward J. Walsh, and Rex H. Warland. 1988. "Differential Paths to Political Activism: Comparisons of Four Mobilization Processes after the Three Mile Island Accident." *Social Forces* 66:951–969. Chapter 8.

Capek, Stella M. 1993. "The 'Environmental Justice' Frame: A Conceptual Discussion and an Application." *Social Problems* 40:5–24. Chapters 8, 9.

————. 1991. "Community, Class, and Contamination: Toxic Waste Protests in Arkansas." Paper presented at the Annual Meetings of the American Sociological Association. Cincinnati: August. Chapter 9.

Carson, Rachel. 1962. *Silent Spring.* Boston: Houghton Mifflin. Chapter 5.

Catton, William. 1980. *Overshoot.* Urbana: University of Illinois Press. Chapter 3.

Commission for Racial Justice. 1987. *Toxic Wastes and Race: A National Report on the Racial and Socioeconomic Characteristics of Communities with Hazardous Wastes Sites.* New York: United Church of Christ. Chapter 7.

Corson, Walter H. 1990. *The Global Ecology Handbook.* Boston: Beacon Press. General Reference.

Cotgrove, Stephen. 1982. *Catastrophe or Cornucopia: The Environment, Politics and the Future.* New York: John Wiley & Sons. Chapters 2, 3, 4.

Couch, Stephen R., and Stephen Kroll-Smith. 1985. "The Chronic Technical Disaster: Toward a Social Scientific Perspective." *Social Science Quarterly* 66:564–575. Chapter 6.

Cribb, Julian. 1991. "What's Up Doc?" *The Australian Magazine,* August 24/25:25–32. Chapter 6.

Delgado, Gary. 1986. *Organizing the Movement: The Roots and Growth of ACORN.* Philadelphia: Temple University Press. Chapters 8, 9.

Dunlap, Riley E., and Angela G. Mertig, eds. 1992. *American Environmentalism: The U.S. Environmental Movement, 1970–1990.* Washington, D.C.: Taylor & Francis. Chapters 5, 6, 7, 8.

Dunlap, Riley E., and Rik Scarce. 1991. "The Polls—Poll Trends: Environmental Problems and Protection." *Public Opinion Quarterly* 55:651–672. Chapters 7, 8.

Edelstein, Michael R. 1988. *Contaminated Communities: The Social and Psychological Impacts of Residential Toxic Exposure.* Boulder, Colo.: Westview Press. Chapters 7, 8.

Editors of Buzzworm Magazine. 1993. *1993 Earth Journal: Environmental Almanac and Resource Directory*. Boulder, Colo.: Buzzworm Books. General Reference.

Ehrlich, Paul R. 1968. *The Population Bomb*. New York: Ballantine Books. Chapter 5.

Ehrlich, Paul R., and Anne H. Ehrlich. 1991. *Healing the Planet*. Reading, Mass.: Addison-Wesley. Chapter 3.

English, Mary R. 1992. *Siting Low-Level Radioactive Waste Disposal Facilities*. Westport, Conn.: Quorum Books. Chapters 3, 7.

Epstein, Edwin M. 1969. *The Corporation in American Politics*. Englewood Cliffs, N.J.: Prentice-Hall. Chapter 4.

Erickson, Brad, ed. 1990. *Call to Action: Handbook for Ecology, Peace and Justice*. San Francisco: Sierra Club Books. General Reference.

Erikson, Kai. 1991. "A New Species of Trouble." Pp. 11–29 in Stephen Robert Couch and J. Stephen Kroll-Smith, eds. *Communities at Risk: Collective Responses to Technological Hazards*. New York: Peter Lang Publishing. Chapter 6.

Ehrlich, Anne H., and John W. Birks, eds. 1990. *Hidden Dangers: Environmental Consequences of Preparing for War*. San Francisco: Sierra Club Books. Chapter 7.

Evans, Sara M., and Harry Boyte. 1986. *Free Spaces: The Sources of Democratic Change in America*. New York: Harper & Row. Chapters 8, 9.

Feagin, Joe R., and Stella M. Capek. 1991. "Grassroots Movements in a Class Perspective." *Research in Political Sociology* 5:27–53. Greenwich, Conn.: JAI Press. Chapter 9.

Feagin, Joe R., and Clairece Booher Feagin. 1990. *Social Problems: A Critical Power-Conflict Perspective*, 3rd ed. Englewood Cliffs, N.J.: Prentice Hall. Chapters 2, 3, 4.

Finsterbusch, Kurt. 1989. "Community Responses to Exposures to Hazardous Wastes." Pp. 57–80 in Dennis L. Peck, ed. *Psychosocial Effects of Hazardous Toxic Waste Disposal on Communities*. Springfield, Ill.: Charles C. Thomas. Chapters 6, 7, 9.

Fisher, Steven, ed. 1993. *Fighting Back in Appalachia: Traditions of Resistance and Change*. Philadelphia: Temple University Press. Chapter 9.

Freudenberg, Nicholas. 1984. *Not in Our Backyards! Community Action for Health and the Environment*. New York: Monthly Review Press. Chapters 6, 7.

Freudenberg, Nicholas, and Carol Steinsapir. 1992. "Not in Our Backyards: The Grassroots Environmental Movement." Pp. 27–38 in Riley E. Dunlap and Angela G. Mertig, eds. *American Environmentalism: The U.S. Environmental Movement, 1970–1990*. Philadelphia: Taylor & Francis. Chapters 6, 7.

Freudenburg, William R. 1992. "Environmental Research." In *Environment, Technology, and Society* 68:1–4. Newsletter of the Section on Environment and Technology, American Sociological Association. Chapter 1.

———. 1985. "Applying Sociology to Policy: Social Science and the Environmental Impact Statement." *Rural Sociology* 50:578–605. Chapter 4.

Fuentes, Marta, and Andre Gunder Frank. 1989. "Ten Theses on Social Movements." *World Development* 17:179–191. Chapter 9.

Gale, Richard P. 1986. "Social Movements and the State: The Environmental Movement, Countermovement, and Government Agencies." *Sociological Perspectives* 29, 2:202–240. Chapter 4.

Gleick, James. 1987. *Chaos: Making a New Science*. New York: Viking Penguin. Chapter 1.

Goldman, Benjamin A. 1991. *The Truth About Where You Live*. New York: Random House.

Gough, Ian. 1979. *The Political Economy of the Welfare State*. London: Macmillan Press Ltd. Chapters 2, 4.

Greider, William. 1992. *Who Will Tell the People: The Betrayal of American Democracy*. New York: Simon & Schuster. Chapters 8, 9.

Greve, Michael S., and Fred L. Smith, eds. 1992. *Environmental Politics*. Westport, Conn.: Praeger Publishers. Chapters 2, 4, 8, 9.

Habermas, Jürgen. 1987. *The Theory of Communicative Action*. Volume 2: *Lifeworld and System: A Critique of Functionalist Reason*. Translated by Thomas McCarthy. Boston: Beacon Press. Chapter 9.

Habermas, Jürgen. 1975. *Legitimation Crisis*. Boston: Beacon Press. Chapter 4.

Hall, Bob, and Mary Lee Kerr. 1991. *1991–1992 Green Index*. Washington, D.C.: Island Press. General Reference.

Hamilton, Lawrence C. 1985. "Concern About Toxic Wastes: Three Demographic Predictors." *Sociological Perspectives* 28:463–486. Chapter 7.

———. 1985. "Who Cares About Water Pollution? Opinions in a Small-Town Crisis." *Sociological Inquiry* 55:170–181. Chapter 7.

Hawkins, Keith. 1984. *Environment and Enforcement: Regulation and the Social Definition of Pollution*. Oxford: Clarendon Press. Chapter 4.

Hays, Samuel P. 1959. *Conservation and the Gospel of Efficiency: The Progressive Conservation Movement, 1890–1920*. Cambridge, Mass.: Harvard University Press. Chapter 5.

Heskin, Allan David. 1991. *The Struggle for Community*. Boulder, Colo.: Westview Press. Chapters 8, 9.

Highlander Research and Education Center. 1992. "Environment and Development in the USA: A Grassroots Report for UNCED." New Market, Tenn.: Highlander Research and Education Center. Chapter 7.

Hoban, Thomas Moore, and Richard Oliver Brooks. 1987. *Green Justice*. Boulder, Colo.: Westview Press. Chapter 3.

Humphrey, Craig R., and Frederick R. Buttel. 1982. *Environment, Energy, and Society*. Belmont, Calif.: Wadsworth. Chapters 2, 5.

Jessop, Bob. 1982. *The Capitalist State: Marxist Theories and Methods*. New York: New York University Press. Chapter 4.

Jessup, Deborah. 1990. *Guide to State Environmental Programs*. Washington, D.C.: Bureau of National Affairs. General Reference.

Kazis, Richard, and Richard L. Grossman. 1982. *Fear at Work: Job Blackmail, Labor and the Environment*. New York: Pilgrim Press. Chapter 4.

Kerbo, Harold R. 1983. *Social Stratification and Inequality: Class Conflict in the United States*. New York: McGraw-Hill. Chapter 4.

Kolko, Gabriel. 1967. *The Triumph of Conservatism*. Chicago: Quadrangle. Chapter 4.

Krauss, Celene. 1989. "Community Struggles and the Shaping of Democratic Consciousness." *Sociological Forum* 4, 2:227–239. Chapter 9.

Kroll-Smith, J. Stephen, and Stephen Robert Couch. 1990. *The Real Disaster Is Above Ground: A Mine Fire and Social Conflict*. Lexington: University Press of Kentucky. Chapter 7.

Kroll-Smith, J. Stephen, and Anthony E. Ladd. 1993. "Environmental Illness and Biomedicine: Anomalies, Exemplars, and the Politics of the Body." *Sociological Spectrum* 13:7–33. Chapters 8, 9.

Lash, Jonathan. 1984. *A Season of Spoils: The Reagan Administration's Attack on the Environment.* New York: Pantheon Books. Chapter 7.

Lenssen, Nicholas. 1992. "Confronting Nuclear Waste." *State of the World 1992,* edited by Linda Starke. New York: W. W. Norton. Chapter 7.

Levine, Adeline. 1982. *Love Canal: Science, Politics, and People.* Lexington, Mass.: Lexington Books, D. C. Heath & Co. Chapter 6.

Lukes, Steven. 1988. *Power: A Radical View.* New York: Macmillan Press. Chapters 2, 4.

Lynd, Robert S. 1957. "Power in American Society as Resource and Problem." Pp. 1–45 in A. Kornhauser, ed. *Problems of Power in American Democracy.* Detroit: Wayne State University Press. Chapter 9.

Manes, Christopher. 1990. *Green Rage: Radical Environmentalism and the Unmaking of Civilization.* Boston: Little, Brown. Chapter 8.

Mann, Dean E., ed. 1981. *Environmental Policy Formation: The Impact of Values, Ideology, and Standards.* Lexington, Mass.: D. C. Heath & Co. Chapter 4.

Marger, Martin N. 1987. *Elites and Masses: An Introduction to Political Sociology.* Belmont, Calif.: Wadsworth. Chapters 2, 4.

Merchant, Carolyn. 1992. *Radical Ecology.* New York: Routledge. Chapters 7, 8.

Milbrath, Lester W. 1984. *Environmentalists: Vanguard for a New Society.* Albany, N.Y.: SUNY Press.

Miller, G. Tyler, Jr. 1988. *Environmental Science: An Introduction.* 2nd ed. Belmont, Calif.: Wadsworth. Chapter 3.

Mitchell, Robert Cameron, Angela G. Mertig, and Riley E. Dunlap. 1992. "Twenty Years of Environmental Mobilization: Trends Among National Environmental Organizations." Pp. 11–26 in Riley E. Dunlap and Angela G. Mertig, eds. *American Environmentalism: The U.S. Environmental Movement, 1970–1990.* Philadelphia: Taylor & Francis. Chapters 6, 7, 8.

Morrison, Denton E. 1986. "How and Why Environmental Consciousness Has Trickled Down." In Allan Schnaiberg and Nicholas Watts, eds. *Distributional Conflicts in Environmental Resource Policy.* Aldershot, England: Gower Publishing Co. Chapters 6, 7, 8.

Morrison, Denton, and Riley Dunlap. 1986. "Environmentalism and Elitism: A Conceptual and Empirical Analysis." *Environmental Management* 10:581–589. Chapter 6.

Nash, Roderick Frazier. 1990. *American Environmentalism: Readings in Conservation History.* 3rd ed. New York: McGraw-Hill. Chapter 5.

Nebel, Bernard J. 1990. *Environmental Science: The Way the World Works.* 3rd ed. Englewood Cliffs, N.J.: Prentice-Hall. Chapter 3.

O'Connor, James. 1973. *The Fiscal Crisis of the State.* New York: St. Martin's Press. Chapter 4.

Olsen, Marvin E., Dora G. Lodwick, and Riley E. Dunlap. 1992. *Viewing the World Ecologically.* Boulder, Colo.: Westview Press. Chapters 7, 8, 9.

Openchowski, Charles. 1990. *A Guide to Environmental Law in Washington, D.C.* Washington, D.C.: Island Press. General Reference.

Piasecki, Bruce, and Peter Asmus. 1990. *In Search of Environmental Excellence: Moving Beyond Blame.* New York: Simon & Schuster. Chapters 7, 8, 9.

Pierce, John C., Mary Ann E. Steger, Brent S. Steel, Nicholas P. Lovrich. 1992. *Citizens, Political Communication and Interest Groups.* Westport, Conn.: Praeger Publishers. Chapters 2, 4.

Piven, Frances Fox, and Richard A. Cloward. 1982. *The New Class War: Reagan's Attack on the Welfare State and Its Consequences.* New York: Pantheon Books. Chapter 7.

Porter, Gareth and Janet Welsh Brown. 1991. *Global Environmental Politics.* Boulder, Colo.: Westview Press. Chapters 4, 7, 8, 9.

Rader, Rebecca L. 1992. "Redemocratizing America: A Comparative Case Study Analysis of Two East Tennessee Community Organizations." Unpublished M.A. thesis, University of Tennessee-Knoxville. Chapters 8, 9.

Raphael, Beverly. 1986. *When Disaster Strikes: How Individuals and Communities Cope with Catastrophe.* New York: Basic Books. Chapter 6.

Redclift, Michael. 1987. *Sustainable Development: Exploring the Contradictions.* London: Methuen. Chapter 3.

Renner, Michael. 1991. "Assessing the Military's War on the Environment." Pp. 132–152 in Lester R. Brown, ed. *State of the World.* New York: W. W. Norton. Chapter 7.

ReVelle, Penelope, and Charles ReVelle. 1992. *The Global Environment: Securing a Sustainable Future.* Boston: Jones and Bartlett Publishers. Chapter 3.

Richardson, Genevra, with Anthony Ogus and Paul Burrows. 1983. *Policing Pollution: A Study of Regulation and Enforcement.* Oxford: Clarendon Press. Chapter 4.

Rodda, Annabel. 1991. *Women and the Environment.* Atlantic Highlands, NJ: Zed. Chapter 6.

Sagoff, Mark, ed. 1988. *The Economy of the Earth: Philosophy, Law and the Environment.* NY: Cambridge University Press. Chapter 3.

Sandbach, Francis. 1980. *Environment, Ideology and Policy.* Oxford: Basil Blackwell. Chapters 2, 4.

Schnaiberg, Allan. 1991. "The Political Economy of Environmental Problems and Policies: Consciousness, Conflict, and Control Capacity." In Riley Dunlap and William Michelson, eds. *Handbook of Environmental Sociology.* Westport, Conn.: Greenwood Press. Chapters 2, 4.

——. 1980. *The Environment: From Surplus to Scarcity.* New York: Oxford University Press. Chapters 1, 2, 3, 4.

Schnaiberg, Allan, Nicholas Watts, and Klaus Zimmerman, eds. 1986. *Distributional Conflicts in Environmental-Resource Policy.* Aldershot, England: Gower Publishing Co. Chapters 2, 4.

Scott, James C. 1990. *Domination and the Arts of Resistance.* New Haven, Conn.: Yale University Press. Chapters 7, 8, 9.

——. 1985. *Weapons of the Weak.* New Haven, Conn.: Yale University Press. Chapters 7, 8, 9.

Shanley, Robert A. 1992. *Presidential Influence and Environmental Policy.* Westport, Conn.: Greenwood Press. Chapter 7.

Shiva, Vandana. 1990. *The Violence of the Green Revolution.* Atlantic Highlands, NJ: Zed Books. Chapter 3.

Shover, Neal, Donald A. Clelland, and John Lynxwiler. 1986. *Enforcement or Negotiation: Constructing a Regulatory Bureaucracy.* Albany: State University of New York Press. Chapters 2, 4.

Shulman, Seth. 1992. *The Threat at Home: Confronting the Toxic Legacy of the U.S. Military.* Boston: Beacon Press. Chapter 7.

Stead, W. Edward, and Jean Garner Stead. 1992. *Management for a Small Planet: Strategic Decision Making and the Environment.* Newbury Park, Calif.: Sage Publications. Chapters 3, 4.

Stone, Christopher. 1975. *Where the Law Ends.* New York: Harper Torchbooks. Chapter 4.

Szymanski, Albert. 1978. *The Capitalist State and the Politics of Class.* Cambridge, Mass.: Winthrop Publishers, Inc. Chapter 4.

Theodorson, George A., and Achilles G. Theodorson. 1969. *A Modern Dictionary of Sociology.* New York: Harper & Row. General Reference.

Thurow, Lester. 1980. *The Zero-Sum Society.* New York: Basic Books. Chapter 7.

Van Voorst, Bruce. 1992. "A Thousand Points of Blight." *Time,* November 9:68–69. Chapter 7.

Walsh, Edward J. 1988. *Democracy in the Shadows: Citizen Mobilization in the Wake of the Accident at Three Mile Island.* Westport, Conn.: Greenwood Press. Chapters 6, 8, 9.

———. 1981. "Resource Mobilization and Citizen Protest in Communities Around Three Mile Island." *Social Problems* 26:1–21. Chapter 6.

Walsh, Edward J., and Rex H. Warland. 1983. "Social Movement Involvement in the Wake of a Nuclear Accident: Activists and Free Riders in the TMI Area." *American Sociological Review* 48:764–780. Chapter 6.

Washburn, Philo, ed. 1992. *Research in Political Sociology.* Greenwich, Conn.: JAI Press. General reference.

West, Guida, and Rhoda Lois Blumberg. 1990. *Women and Social Protest.* New York: Oxford University Press. Chapter 8.

White, Lynn, Jr. 1967. "The Historical Roots of Our Ecological Crisis." *Science* 155:1203–1207. Chapter 5.

Wolfe, Alan. 1977. *The Limits of Legitimacy: Political Contradictions of Contemporary Capitalism.* New York: Free Press. Chapter 4.

Yeager, Peter C. 1987. "Structural Bias in Regulatory Law Enforcement: The Case of the U.S. Environmental Protection Agency." *Social Problems* 34:330–344. Chapter 4.

Zisk, Betty H. 1992. *The Politics of Transformation.* Westport, Conn.: Praeger Publishers. General reference.

List of Environmental Organizations

Acid Rain Foundation
1410 Varsity Drive
Raleigh, N.C. 27606

Alliance to Save Energy
1725 K Street, N.W./914
Washington, D.C. 20006–1401

American Conservation Association
30 Rockefeller Plaza/5402
New York, N.Y. 10112

American Forestry Association
1516 P Street, N.W.
Washington, D.C. 20036

American Hiking Society
P.O. Box 20160
Washington, D.C. 20041–2160

American Solar Energy Society
850 West Morgan Street
Raleigh, N.C. 27603

Beyond Beef
1130 17th Street, N.W./300
Washington, D.C. 20036

Carrying Capacity
1325 G Street, N.W./1003
Washington, D.C. 20005

Center for Economic Conversion
222 View Street
Mountain View, Calif. 94305

Center for Environmental Information
46 Prince Street
Rochester, N.Y. 14607

Center for Marine Conservation
1725 DeSales Street, N.W./500
Washington, D.C. 20036

Chesapeake Bay Foundation
162 Prince George Street
Annapolis, Md. 21401

Citizens Clearinghouse for Hazardous Waste
(Center for Environmental Justice)
P.O. Box 926
Arlington, Va. 22216

Citizens for Ocean law
1601 Connecticut Avenue, N.W./202
Washington, D.C. 20009

Clean Water Action
1320 18th Street, N.W./300
Washington, D.C. 20036

Coalition on Superfund
1730 Pennsylvania Avenue, N.W./200
Washington, D.C. 20006

Common Cause
2030 M Street, N.W.
Washington, D.C. 20036

Sources: This list of environmental organizations was compiled from a number of sources, most notably Ilana Kotin, ed., *1993 Earth Journal: Environmental Almanac and Resource Directory* (Boulder, Colo.: Buzzworm Books, 1993); and Walter H. Corson, ed., *Global Ecology Handbook* (Boston: Beacon Press, 1990).

The Conservation Foundation
1250 24th Street, N.W./500
Washington, D.C. 20037

Co-op America
2100 M. Street, N.W./310
Washington, D.C. 20036

Council on Economic Priorities
30 Irving Place
New York, N.Y. 10003

Council for Solid Waste Solutions
1275 K Street, N.W./400
Washington, D.C. 20005

The Cousteau Society, Inc.
870 Greenbrier Circle/402
Chesapeake, Va. 23320

Defenders of Wildlife
1244 19th Street, N.W.
Washington, D.C. 20036

Earth Island Institute
300 Broadway/28
San Francisco, Calif. 94133

Earthwatch
P.O. Box 403N
Watertown, Mass. 02172

Environmental Defense Fund
1616 P Street, N.W./150
Washington, D.C. 20036

The Environmental Exchange
1930 18th Street, N.W./24
Washington, D.C. 20009

Environmental Policy Institute
218 D Street, S.E.
Washington, D.C. 20003

Friends of the Earth
218 D Street, S.E.
Washington, D.C. 20003

Global Tomorrow Coalition
1325 G Street N.W./915
Washington, D.C. 20005–3014

Greenpeace USA
Main Office
1436 U Street, N.W.
Washington, D.C. 20009

Institute for Earth Education
Cedar Cove
Greenville, W.Va. 24945

Izaak Walton League
1701 North Ft. Myer Drive/1100
Arlington, Va. 22209

The Land and Water Fund of the Rockies
2260 Baseline/200
Boulder, Colo. 80302

League of Conservation Voters
1707 L Street, N.W./550
Washington, D.C. 20036

National Audubon Society
950 Third Avenue
New York, N.Y. 10022

National Clean Air Coalition
801 Pennsylvania Avenue, S.E.
Washington, D.C. 20003

National Coalition Against the Misuse of Pesticides
701 E Street, S.E./200
Washington, D.C. 20003

National Recycling Coalition
P.O. Box 80729
Lincoln, Nebr. 68729

National Toxics Campaign
1168 Commonwealth Avenue
Boston, Mass. 02134

National Wildlife Federation
1400 16th Street, N.W.
Washington, D.C. 20036

Natural Resources Defense Council
1350 New York Avenue, N.W./300
Washington, D.C. 20005

The Nature Conservancy
1815 North Lynn Street
Arlington, Va. 22209

Nuclear Information and Resource Service
1424 16th Street, N.W./601
Washington, D.C. 20036

Rainforest Alliance
295 Madison Avenue/1804
New York, N.Y. 10017

Renew America
1400 16th Street, N.W./710
Washington, D.C. 20036

Sierra Club
408 C Street, N.E.
Washington, D.C. 20002

Southwest Network for Environmental and Economic Justice
P.O. Box 7399
Albuquerque, N.Mex. 87194

20/20 Vision
30 Cottage Street
Amherst, Mass. 01002

Wilderness Society
1400 I Street, N.W./10th Floor
Washington, D.C. 20005

Women's Environment and Development Organization
845 Third Avenue/15th Floor
New York, N.Y. 10022

Working Group on Community Right to Know
215 Pennsylvania Avenue S.E.
Washington, D.C. 20003

World Resources Institute
1709 New York Avenue, N.W./700
Washington, D.C. 20006

Worldwatch Institute
1776 Massachusetts Avenue N.W.
Washington, D.C. 20036

World Wildlife Fund
1250 24th Street, N.W./500
Washington, D.C. 20037

Zero Population Growth
1400 16th Street, N.W./3rd Floor
Washington, D.C. 20036

Index

Waste disposal, 32, 35, 75–84
    deep well injection, 35
    hazardous wastes, 32
    landfills, 35
    Love Canal, 75–84
    midnight dumping, 35

    solid wastes, 32
    surface impoundments, 35
    toxic chemical wastes, 32
Withdrawals to the environment, 20
World War II, 60–61